"Mom, You Don't Understand!"

A Daughter and Mother Share Their Views

by Carol Koffinke and
daughter Julie Jordan

DEACONESS PRESS
Minneapolis, Minnesota

Published by Deaconess Press (a service of Fairview Riverside
Medical Center, a division of Fairview Hospital and Healthcare
Services), 2450 Riverside Avenue South, Minneapolis, MN 55454

Library of Congress Cataloging-in-Publication Data

Koffinke, Carol.
    Mom, you don't understand! : a daughter and mother share their
views / by Carol Koffinke and Julie Jordan.
        p.   cm.
    Summary: A mother and daughter take turns explaining their
perspectives on twenty-seven issues which commonly cause
disagreements, including family relationships, self-image,
friendship, and love.
    ISBN 0-925190-66-7 (pbk.) : $8.95
    1. Mothers and daughters--United States--Juvenile literature.
2. Teenage girls--United States--Juvenile literature.   [1. Mothers
and daughters. 2. Conduct of life.]   I. Jordan, Julie.   II. Title.
HQ755.85.K63   1993
306.874'3--dc20   93-17216
                                                                             CIP
                                                                              AC

First printing: May, 1993

Printed in the United States of America
97 96 95 94 93   7 6 5 4 3 2 1

Cover design by Susan Kroese

to daughters
...for every mother has been a daughter

Contents

Self-Image

Friends

Love

Acknowledgments

Julie and I wish to thank a number of people for their assistance and support while writing our book.

First of all, Julie would like to thank her stepsister Heather for her openness in discussing the intensity of problems Julie's personal experience did not encompass. She would also like to thank her special friend Jim for a male perspective on the "boy" issues.

Carol would like to express her gratitude to her husband Dick and son Richard, who both provided support, unselfish encouragement, and enthusiasm for both the writing and the anticipated publication of this book. She also would like to express her admiration and appreciation to her mother Shirley, whose love paved the way for the next generation of her family's mothers and daughters. Many thanks to her sisters Eva, Julie, Janet, and Chris, who shared her experiences as a daughter and now share her experiences as a mother. Finally, Carol would like to thank the many women who have touched her life, either through friendship or as patients. Many, many lessons have been learned.

Together we would like to acknowledge each other for the honesty and determination it took to work together in understanding and interpreting the many issues involved, even in our own relationship.

And both of us would like to thank God for being there all the way.

Introduction

Julie and I would like to welcome you to our book. If you are a teen daughter, you will have an opportunity to read not only what amounts to a diary from a fellow teenage girl, but also the diary of her mother. Don't feel guilty—that was our intent. If you are a mom, you can read a teenage girl's diary without being sneaky or dishonest, as well as that of a fellow pilgrim in the realm of mothering a teenage girl.

The book covers twenty-seven topics, each of which has three short pieces attached to it. The first is written by Julie and includes her innermost thoughts and feelings on the subject at hand. We knew it would be counterproductive to censor her anger and other feelings, so she really let them rip.

The second piece is where I allowed myself to indulge the thoughts and feelings of being a mom without worrying if I was being irrational, silly, or selfish. (And I can tell you now, I was all of the above at times.)

The third piece is an impartial look at the real issues beneath the situations, behaviors and feelings. It attempts to clarify why the situation occurs, why it is difficult for both parties, and how mothers and daughters can work together to resolve it, or at least survive the crisis when it is caused by something out of their control—such as a boy cheating on a daughter.

Writing the book and analyzing the various issues made the cause of the conflicts that are so common between parents and teenagers crystal clear to us. Julie and I realized there are two major shifts which occur simultaneously—but in opposite directions—during the teenage years. The first and most obvious is the shift teenagers make from dependence to independence. This involves the teen accepting more responsibility, making her own decisions, developing her own opinions, and emerging from the protective wings of her parents. She is moving from child to adult.

At the same time, however, the parent is having to shift in the opposite direction—from protector/teacher/dictator to a role which basically gives up control of the child. This is a gradual process, but a scary one. It means stepping back and trusting that what the mother has tried to teach has been absorbed and will be applied to the many situations the teen will find herself facing. What is frightening is that the parent can't be there anymore—saying yes or no, do or don't, now or later. Also, because the teenager is developing a sense of who she is, opinions, goals, values, and perceptions emerge which may vary from the parent's. This is normal—parents haven't yet learned how to clone themselves.

Sometimes the variance from what was taught and what the teen verbalizes is so great, parents panic that the teen is "going astray," so they jump in to gain control again. They don't realize that the teen is experimenting with a variety of ideas which will change frequently before settling in. She may need to establish her individuality, and some sense of rebellion is sometimes necessary to help propel her forward.

This "push-off" from the parent can be very frightening for both parties, and both shifts are difficult. The role that the parent has become accustomed to is transforming itself, whether they want it to or not. The role of child that teens have previously become accustomed to is also transforming itself whether they want it to or not, because the role of child is no longer sufficient in their lives. Yet they aren't quite sure how to be an adult.

In working through these issues with Julie, I've learned a lot about her. We now realize we are faced with the development of her self-image, which is separate from mine. I've also learned a lot about myself and my feelings as a mother, which could never have been conveyed strictly from my "therapist" point of view.

When we started to write, we made a list of issues that tend to be difficult for the teen, and subsequently can cause tension between daughters and mothers. Maybe the issue involves the mother, or it's one where the daughter is upset and doesn't know how to communicate her feelings. Or perhaps she is going through a difficult time and her mother doesn't know how to support her. The topics we chose cover all three instances, and are some of the most common and troublesome sources of conflict between the two generations.

Daughters can read this book and get validation for feelings which they may think seem silly or selfish at times. They can gain insight into why mom is responding the way she does. Then, they can use the suggestions offered on ways to ease the tension.

Moms can read Julie's pieces and get a sense of the uncertainty, insecurity, and confusion that always exists to some degree during the teen years. They can gain insight into what is behind behavior that often hides the truth or distracts from it. They can receive validation for their feelings of fear, helplessness, and frustration when attempts to communicate love for their daughters end in arguments, slammed doors, or isolation. Then they can face the problems and find solutions in the third piece.

All mothers and daughters aren't alike, but the struggles are pretty universal—and so are the feelings underneath. Mothers and daughters can sit down and discuss the issues. Encouraging communication is a theme of this book, but the key to resolving arguments is to discuss the *real* issues—not simply addressing the fact that a daughter stayed out until midnight, but also dealing with the transition that both mother and the daughter are experiencing. Anger is often only a cover-up for fear or hurt.

Julie and I are very proud of this book. Mother/daughter relationships can be so beautiful and special. We know that firsthand, and wish to share this discovery with all our readers.

A Special Note to Teens

I wanted to let the teenagers reading this book understand, teen to teen, *my* motivation for writing it.

We've all had those times, some more often than others, when we would have really liked to discuss our problems with our moms. Unfortunately, either because we *think* that our mother is really unreasonable or she really *is* unreasonable, we either turn to our friends or the problem is ignored. As much as we'd like to think that our friends can help us handle our problems perfectly, they can't. No friend has the knowledge or experience to give good advice on most important subjects, regardless of what we may believe. Most mothers *are* capable of this, but some are not great at sharing their experience in helpful ways. While this hasn't been a problem with my mother, there are times when my problems really scare her and keep her from being as helpful as she could be. I'm not talking about the little ones (like getting a "D" on a test), but important topics, like sex.

Some subjects are harder to talk about than others and that is the motivation for me writing this book—to expose *both* mothers and daughters to each other's reasoning behind their attitudes. My hope is that understanding why we can seem to be so unreasonable to each other will help mothers and daughters become more open-minded. Once we're ready to listen to the other's side, we can use the "resolution page" (the third piece of each topic). After exploring each other's point of view, an understanding can be reached that will improve the status of this complicated mother/daughter relationship and get the problem solved.

Good luck! Please remember that nobody cares more about you than your parents. You and your mother have the potential for the most beautiful relationship. Work hard to love, respect, and understand each other, and your teenage life will become so much easier. There's nothing like the feeling of knowing that *no matter what,* your mother will always be there (this can help get you through the times when no one else is there). You need that mother of yours—I'd die without mine.

Family Issues

"My Parents Expect Too Much"

"I'm sorry. I don't have thirty hands and I cannot be in thirty places at one time. I do the best I can. I get good grades, I'm not a drug addict, I pick good friends, and I'm basically a good kid, right? I *cannot* come home everyday after school (which is tiring enough by itself) and jump up and make everybody happy all of the time. I am in very hard classes and the amount of homework I have is outrageous.

"I can't do this anymore. I want to be able to do everything and Mom and Dad want me to be able to do everything, but I just can't. I'm worn out. Sports make me tired all of the time, homework gets old, and then Mom and Dad walk in the door and the *first* thing they do is complain about the things that *haven't* been done. *Never* how good the things are that *have* been done.

"They want me to be involved in school, so I'm in sports. They want me to get good grades, so I work my butt off. They say they want me to have a social life, so I try to have friends who also require a lot of time. They want me to help around the house, so I do chores.

3

"I want all of these things too, but something has got to give. My body can't do all of this. It's too much, and Mom and Dad don't help me at all. I feel like I am spread so thin! Everyone pulls at my capabilities, and I can't stretch any further.

"I feel like just sitting on my butt and seeing if anyone notices the difference. I doubt they would. Already nobody notices or appreciates *anything* I do. I do so much to help, but I feel like I get nothing in return. They just want more, more, more."

"I'm Worn Out"

"If I walk through the front door one more time after work to such a pig sty I think I'll *scream.* I work hard all day and I don't ask much of her. I think I would drop over dead if she ever helped out without being asked, nagged, or yelled at. Sometimes I wonder if she really cares about me as a person or just sees me as a chauffeur, short order cook, and laundress.

"She's old enough now to be aware of what needs to be done and what her responsiblities are. But everything else comes first, including talking on the phone. I can't help but take it personally when she doesn't keep up with her end of the responsibilities. Helping me seems to be the last item on her list.

"And I *hate* nagging. What I really want to do when I come home from work is talk to her while I fix dinner and hear what happened in her day. But the first thing that grabs me is that she left a mess or didn't do what she was supposed to do.

"True, I expect her to get good grades, but that isn't what keeps her from helping out. It's important for her to learn

5

that responsibilities are a part of life and certain things have to be done before we play.

"I wish we could just work together as a family. We all see what needs to be done and we should help each other out. I could do the dishes for her when she has a lot of homework, and she could help with dinner when I've had a rough day.

"I hate it that everything out of my mouth is "Did you do this? Don't forget to... Why didn't you...?" Sometimes it seems our conversations are restricted to this bantering back and forth. I know it turns her off when I nag, but I get so frustrated sometimes. I wish she could step into my shoes and feel what it's like to have to beg for help.

"She says I pressure her to be too much. God, I hope that's not true. I want her to be the best she can be and sometimes the only way to help her seems to be to nag her. That's not the way I want to be, though. I really just want to love her, enjoy her, and support her but I also have the responsibility of teaching her the basics of survival. Sometimes that part really isn't much fun."

Are Mom and Dad Asking Too Much?

As a mother, I feel lucky if my daughter tells me she is feeling pressured and overwhelmed. These emotions can be very strong, and if they are kept back they can break out as a barrage of statements that make me feel like I'm being blamed for every problem Julie has ever had. Then resentments can form, and the situation is only made worse for both of us.

The real challenge for mothers is to try not to become defensive as they listen to their daughters. This is much easier said than done, because a mother's natural response is often to interrupt and bring the daughter back to reality as a parent defines it. When this happens, however, the communication that is needed gets cut off. The teen might respond by saying something like, "Oh, sure. You only want me to 'communicate' when we're talking about what's important to *you*."

Instead of interrupting, mothers need to honestly consider the validity of what their daughters are saying. Moms need to ask themselves if they are not being insensitive to their daughters' gruelling schedules. At the same time, teens need to ask themselves if they are exaggerating the pressures on them because their feelings of being overwhelmed are so strong at that moment.

Mothers need to think about whether they are able to let go of the demand that chores be completed no matter what is going on at the time. They also need to examine how important it is to them for their daughters to be honor students, top athletes, and popular among their peers, and how much pressure they might be placing on them to be any or all of these things.

Daughters also need to think about their priorities. What goals have they chosen for themselves, and how much pressure has mom really put on them? Sometimes teens can feel like their parents are to blame when they have actually placed the pressure on themselves.

Both mothers and daughters need to know that it's great when daughters want to be in advanced classes, play sports, be president of a club, have a part in the school play, or all of the above. But these are choices that come with consequences. It may help to consider giving up an activity, and in order to do that, daughters must decide which one is least important to them and receive guidance and support from their parents.

When helping daughters make these decisions, parents must keep in mind that during these years, social activities are important. Teens need to work with and develop relationships with peers, both male and female. So it will help if mom accepts that friends and social functions have an important place in the list of priorities. Teens must learn that work comes before play, but work doesn't exclude play, either.

While it is important to be responsible, we're all human and all need a break sometimes.

If feelings of being pressured or overwhelmed aren't talked about, they can come out by such actions as slamming doors or stomping feet. Parents can be afraid to ask what is wrong, and teens may be reluctant to tell their parents what they're feeling. Still, someone must break the ice, and the other side must be open to talking about the problem. The feelings will not go away, and if no one opens up, the distance between parents and daughters becomes wider. Teens need to know that they have someone to talk to about their problems, and parents need to give them a safe place to honestly express their feelings. This means that daughters must make an attempt to communicate, and mothers must be willing to look at themselves and any part they may have played in the problem as they listen.

A Daughter's View _____

"My Parents Are Too Strict"

"**I** didn't know my house would become a prison and that my parents would turn out to be evil guards over my my entire life. There are a few areas even I agree they should be strict about, but this is totally crazy! I ask to go to a party and I can't go unless my friend's parents are going to be in the room the *entire* time. When I ask to go somewhere with friends, if the answer isn't a flat out "no," I have to explain the times, transportation arrangements, and especially the company I'm going to be keeping. My curfew is completely unfair and no matter what I say they don't see anything wrong in what they're doing.

"Mom thinks that since she's my parent, she should be entitled to whatever restrictions she pleases. Great! But since she is my parent, isn't she also supposed to want me to be happy? How can she possibly expect me to be happy when she makes it perfectly obvious that she doesn't even want me to leave the house? She's still living in the dark ages—this is the 90s! She can't always be there making every decision for me.

"She says she trusts *me*, but not my limited experience.

How in the world can she possibly expect me to *get* experience when I can't leave the house without the third degree?

"I really dread asking her if I can do anything, even something simple that all of my friends are automatically allowed to do, because I know I'm going to be in for the interrogation of the century. At this rate I'll never grow up. Does she want me to stay a kid forever?"

"It's a Dangerous World Out There"

"She's mad at me again. I try to set reasonable limits, curfews, and guidelines, but I'm constantly accused of being too strict and overprotective.

"She has much more freedom and many more privileges than I had when I was a teenager, but it never seems to be enough. Sometimes it feels like the only arrangement that would suit her would be for her to briefly check in once a week with me—just long enough to let me know she's alive. She resents it when I ask reasonable questions like where she's going and who she's going with, who is driving, what they will be doing, and when she'll be home.

"I know it's a tough world out there. There are drugs readily available in our schools and communities. Many teens drink and drive. There is date rape, car-jacking, cults. Am I wrong to try to make sure that she will be reasonably safe when she is out on her own?

"She accuses me of not trusting her, but it really has nothing to do with trusting her. I'm afraid of her being put in a situation where she hasn't had the experience necessary to protect herself. When I see her walk out the door with friends, at night, in cars, she just looks so vulnerable.

"Would she be able to confront her friends and say, "I'm not driving with you—you've been drinking," "Slow down, you're driving too fast," "I don't care for any cocaine, thank you," or "Please get your hand off my butt."? I know how hard it is to say these things to other kids, and I'm so afraid she'll end up someone's victim.

"I don't want to lose my little girl. True, it's hard to see her grow up, but what I'm really afraid of is that she'll be killed, raped, or fall victim to some other tragedy. I've got to protect her the best I can."

The Transfer of Control

The battle of wills is bound to be fought off and on between mother and daughter during the teenage years. One area where this battle is often engaged is that of rules. Teens often see themselves as more grown up than their parents see them, and they want the rights and privileges that go along with the status of an adult. On the other hand, as parents have played the role of sole commander for quite a few years, they tend to feel insecure in letting go of some of their control. It is quite understandable that conflict results.

The mission for the teenager is to move smoothly into the role of an independent adult. A nicely paced transition from childhood to adulthood allows them to learn and practice new skills as their autonomy increases gradually.

A smooth transition for parents, on the other hand, involves moving slowly into a role which is less controlling. Their mission is to allow the teen to experience more and more independence as they demonstrate that they are ready to do so.

It would be silly to expect someone who had just finished

sixth grade to be equipped to make all of his or her own decisions. They would not be equipped to handle the many new situations they had never encountered before. They would probably feel unsure of themselves and end up making mistakes that could be quite costly.   On the other hand, parents who have been responsible for making just about every decision for their child since birth, would feel very insecure if they were expected to suddenly give up complete jurisdiction over that child. This would be a very frightening feeling, and cause constant worry.

Personally, I know that when Julie has asked to do something new and different, like traveling someplace with a teen driver or participating in an all-night roller-skating party, my first impulse has usually been to say no. But when I've allowed myself to step back and look at my initial response, I've realized it has often been made out of fear. When she asks me to sanction some unprecedented request, my gut tends to contract and my mouth unthinkingly says no. To be honest, it is easier to say no than to consider her request thoughtfully, because the situation often seems to expand the borders of her autonomy at an uncomfortably fast rate.

Mothers would do better to think for awhile before they make a decision in cases when permission must be given for their daughter to enter unchartered territory. Sometimes it helps to say something like, "I'd like to talk that over with your Dad," which at least buys some time. (If the father usually takes an active role in raising the daughter, this small postponement is a good move in any case.) This timeout helps a mother sort out exactly what it is she is afraid of.

It's much better to face the fact that the unfamiliar prospect is frightening than to deny it and become rigid. After coming to some conclusions about what her reservations are to the new request, mom can sit down with her daughter and explain what concerns her about the situation. The mother can allow her daughter to answer the questions she needs to have answered, and this information will enable her to feel safe enough to either give her permission or to decide that the risks are too great to say yes.

Daughters need to understand that each new request pulls her mother into unfamiliar territory where she really isn't sure what is and isn't o.k. There are no precedents, so mom isn't sure what the boundaries, limits, and rules should be. If the daughter can offer as much information as possible to allow her mother to gain a pretty good picture of what the situation is going to entail, she will most likely meet with less resistance.

When Julie is patient with me as I ask the questions that I need to ask in order to feel confident that the situation is safe for her, I appreciate it. Sometimes she even precedes her request with an explanation of all the details which lets me know that she is aware of my concerns and respects my feelings. To expect me to blindly say yes to all of her requests and then become outraged with me when I don't would only confirm immaturity on her part and increase my doubts about her ability to handle a new responsibility.

If there are rules currently in place that seem unreasonable, they may need to be renegotiated. Perhaps a 10:00 curfew was fine when the daughter was thirteen, but as she matures, this needs to be reexamined.

A daughter can have an edge in these negotiations if she has been able to demonstrate responsibility in managing rules in the past. If she stuck to her previous curfew over a period of time, then she has shown evidence of a degree of maturity. With each year a daughter has many opportunities to show good judgment, and the more she can act in ways that show she can make responsible decisions and use good judgment, the less fearful mom will be as her daughter ventures out on her own.

If Mom isn't willing to move forward, her daughter can give specific examples of times when she has shown good judgment, which will weaken the argument against giving something new a try. If she hasn't shown good judgment in the past, however, the mother will be very hesitant to allow her more independence, believing that her daughter still needs her protection to remain safe.

It is important for both mothers and daughters to listen to each other. Mothers must listen to each situation independently, not rushing into a "no" response because the circumstance is new. And if the daughter is willing to listen to her mother's concerns and provide the necessary information that will allow mom to feel secure in the situation, she will have much better luck in getting affirmative answers. Of course, assuring her mother that she is ready to undertake a new experience needs to be coupled with actions on the part of the daughter that demonstrate a growing sense of responsibility and good judgment. Just as she would expect her mother to follow through with actions when she says something like, "I'll never read your diary again," the daughter must follow through with actions which demonstrate the ability to be responsible and reliable. Both mother and daughter should remember that the need to be strict and say "no" is usually a response to fear. Whatever daughters can do to alleviate their parents' fear will help them achieve more freedom.

"My Parents Are So Tight With Money"

"**I**'m just a kid—I'm not old enough to provide everything for myself. Why did they even have kids if they want me to grow up and be an adult right away? That's the only way I'd be able to afford everything I need for myself. You don't just have a kid and then say, 'Okay, that's that. Now she's on her own.'

"I'm sorry they didn't get anything for free when they were kids. I'm sorry they had to earn absolutely everything they got. But that's not my fault, and I shouldn't be punished for it. Believe me, if I could, I'd give *them* everything they needed to be happy.

"I'm not asking for everything, just a little give and take. Besides clothing, shelter and food, I feel like I'm basically in this world alone. It's not like I don't work hard. I'm so sick of doing so much work in school and so many chores at home and never getting any rewards for any of it. I feel like failing every class, quitting school, and getting a job just so that I can have some of the things I want.

"I *hate* feeling like I don't deserve things that are good in life. That's exactly how they make me feel—whether they're aware of it or not—when they say things like, 'We don't see you working around the house,' or 'You don't seem to care enough about that for us to pay for it.' Well, I'm sorry. By the time I finish my homework (which is a way of *working* toward making it in life and making them happy), playing sports, and practicing music, there is very little time left.

"At my age, I don't think it's fair for me to be expected to get a job just because I want things that everyone else gets automatically. How do you think it makes me feel when all of my friends are talking about their CD players or clothes or other things that they get, and I know I can't even mention wanting them without getting some huge lecture on responsibility?"

"I Have to Teach Her Responsibility"

"What am I? A walking money machine? I'm so sick of having every conversation with her begin with something along the lines of, 'Mom, can I have...?' In case she hasn't noticed, my purse isn't a bottomless pit.

"I can't help the fact that some of her friends get new cars for their birthdays or get summer trips to Spain. We do the best we can, but we're not even close to being wealthy. And even if we were, I don't think it's good to have everything handed to you on a silver platter. That's just not how life works. I think I'd be setting her up for a huge disappointment if I gave her the impression that all you needed to do was ask for something and you could get it. When she has to go out and make it on her own, it would be a harsh realization for her to find out that she will have to work for what she gets.

"She does work hard at school and is responsible in many ways. But when I offer her special projects around the house to earn some extra money, she doesn't seem interested. Yet when she wants that new dress, shoes, coat, or a trip, she expects me to deliver. I'm willing to give her a small allowance and a little entertainment money, but it seems to me that if she wants some special things she should be willing to contribute something in exchange for them.

"Part of me feels guilty when she wants something and I say no. She is a good kid, and I love to see her happy. But I also have to teach her that most of the things we want require some payment—either money or work. We didn't have this problem when she was younger. What she wanted was a lot cheaper, and small children aren't supposed to have to work for what they get. But she's growing up, and that means taking on more responsibility. She asks to be considered an adult when she wants to do something which requires more independence, but then she feels I'm unreasonable for expecting her to assume some responsiblity in getting the things she wants. If I could see some sign that she doesn't expect to have everything given to her, I might feel more generous.

"I know she's at a tough age. She's too young to get a real job, yet many of her tastes are becoming more mature and therefore more expensive. I really hate feeling like a 'tightwad.'"

Financial Dependence
vs. Independence

M oney issues between parents and teens are another aspect of the transitional state of adolescence. The teenager can't work at most jobs because she is going to school, and she isn't old enough to have an after school job until she is over sixteen years of age. Yet her needs become more expensive.

Entertainment and social activities increase, as does the cost of such activities. Daughters are no longer satisfied with patent leather shoes from a discount store. They want yearbooks, prom clothes, and stereo equipment. The emphasis on designer clothes, coupled with an adolescent's need to look like her friends, can hike up clothing expenses considerably.

Whereas a bar of soap and inexpensive shampoo were all the personal care items she needed at age eight, now she needs special shampoo, conditioners, mousse, hairspray, deodorant, lotions, perfume, makeup, and feminine products. When her daughter was small, mom could cut her bangs and trim her hair without any fuss. Now this task has to be performed in a salon, and how about a manicure while they're at it? So here is this teenage girl who has all the material wants and needs of a woman, with no way to create an income to acquire these things.

Mom might be able to understand this feeling if she imagined having her own financial status drastically changed for the worse. Maybe she is used to buying a new dress every couple of months, going out to dinner every so often, having her hair done in her favorite salon on a regular basis, treating the family to steak once in a while, or treating herself to her favorite cologne when she runs out. If she imagines suddenly having to live with never being able to buy anything but hamburger, no entertainment, do-it-yourself haircuts, and cologne from Woolworth's, she might find she would feel unsure of herself, and even somewhat inadequate. What this exercise brings to light is the fact that self-worth can be strongly affected by our material possessions.

Teenage girls have usually not had a strong financial base and then lost it, but they are experimenting with a new role—that of an adult. Their tastes and interests are maturing, yet they have no way to support themselves.

Still, the teenage years are an important time for developing attitudes about work, money, and responsibility. If mom continues to provide everything for her daughter as if she were a child, she will remain childlike in her expectations. Mom has the responsibility to teach her daughter that the older we get, the more we have to earn what we receive. This never sounds like much fun to a daughter who wants to be considered mature when she asks to go on a long trip with some friends, but isn't so keen on that role when she wants "stuff."

As hokey as it sounds, however, there is a feeling of satisfaction that comes along with earning or working for what we get. Having mom pay for dad's birthday gift and marking the gift from her daughter isn't the same as the daughter earning the money herself and buying the gift for dad.

Moms need to understand, however, that this is a hard in-between stage for teenagers. Daughters may see their mothers take their friends to lunch, buy things for themselves when they want them (at least from the daughter's perspective), and go out to dinner or a movie whenever they want. The daughter isn't privy to mom's inner discussion, in which she asks herself, "Can I afford this now?" or "Should I wait until next month?" So mom's outward behavior becomes her daughter's model for adult behavior.

Mothers and daughter should discuss an arrangement that seems reasonable for the two of them based on family income and beliefs. In doing this, there are several specific questions to consider. Should mom give her daughter a small allowance but also pay for the necessities (including personal items and clothes), or should she give her a larger allowance and expect her to manage all her own purchases? What kind and amount of work is fair to expect for what amount of money? Should there be a limit on entertainment expenses per week so that the daughter will always understand the amount of money she has available and can plan accordingly? Can mom provide her daughter with opportunities to earn extra money for Christmas and birthdays until she is old enough to work? Or if she is old enough, is it practical or desirable for her to work outside of the home? As you can see, this is a complicated subject.

What won't help is for mom to call her daughter a demanding brat and for daughter to call mom a tightwad. Open communication is needed, not name calling.

"Mom's Always Too Busy For Me"

"Why did she even bother having me in the first place? Did she think she'd just have a kid and that's it? No more responsibilities? Oh sure, she realized she'd have to feed me, clothe me, and give me shelter, but other than that, did she think she could leave me on my own?

"Am I not important to her at all? If I am, you sure wouldn't know it from this end. My mother is never here! It's like she has her own life and I'm not included in it. My only companions are my friends, and then she wonders why I don't come to her with my problems. It's because I'm afraid she'll just say, "Oh, that's nice, dear. Well, I have to go now." I can't even get two minutes of time in her busy schedule to get help on my homework. She's never home, and half the time I could be dying somewhere and she wouldn't have a clue.

"Why doesn't she love me? (She can't even try to say she does, because if you love someone you try and make time for them in your life.) I don't think there is any way you can make a child feel any more unwanted and unloved than by ignoring him or her. I couldn't feel any emptier knowing that my own mother doesn't care enough to spend one evening at home to catch up with her child."

"I'm Overcommitted"

"I'm feeling super guilty. I know I haven't been home much lately. My job seems to be requiring more and more time, plus there have been a rash of other commitments in the evenings: meetings, dinners, friends with problems. I really haven't been home much at all, and I know she's feeling neglected.

"Sometimes I think I do lose sight of my priorities. At the moment when I tell someone, "Yes, I'll be on that committee," or, "Sure, I can attend that function," each individual commitment seems like no big deal. But what happens is that they all seem to come up at once, and there I am, committed almost every evening of the week after working all day.

"It also seems like there are weeks when she doesn't seem to need me at all anymore. I don't understand her homework well enough to help her with that very much, and my feeble attempts have gotten her more wrong answers than right ones. Now she usually calls her friends when she needs help. Then the rest of her night is spent on the phone or over a neighborhood friend's house.

"It seems like whenever I do get myself overcommitted is when she wants me around to talk to or to help her with something. She will always come first with me, but it's so hard to tell when I'm going to be needed. I really want to be there when those times hit, especially since they are so few and far between anymore. I really don't want to miss them.

"Yet I also realize that she is becoming more and more independent, which means she needs me less and less. Even when I don't overcommit myself, I need to start establishing a life of my own, since the role of mother seems to be taking less and less of my time.

"When she was small I spent most of my day filling her needs—needs that were easy to recognize and fulfill: wet diapers, hunger, boredom, baths, tuck-ins, stories, playing games, and fixing her hair. Now she doesn't need me to do much of anything for her except to drive her here and there. It's hard to know when to be there and when not to.

"Sometimes I feel really tired. There are so many people who seem to want a piece of my time—a piece of me. Time really is the most valuable thing I have right now, and I don't seem to get any of it for myself.

"As the most valuable gift I have, I would gladly give my time to her. If I knew when she wanted it, I would gladly put other activities aside. If I knew she wanted me, I would be there."

Changing Needs

Sometimes mothers can get caught up in a flurry of exhausting commitments which can alienate them from their families. With all of the demands placed on them, there is pressure for modern day mothers to play the role of "Super Mom." To some that means becoming a homemaker's model of perfection—keeping a perfect house, making perfect meals, baking for the community, having perfectly dressed children, and fulfilling all of the family's needs. For others it might mean working an eight to ten hour day, coming home and fixing a three course meal, throwing in a load of clothes before the PTA meeting, volunteering for membership chairman, and scrambling to take care of all the other tasks that need doing. Somewhere within this frenzy of activity is a family.

"Super Moms" sometimes get caught up in the outside appearance of having everything perfect and completing all their tasks only to lose track of the inner workings of what being a mother is all about. By that I mean they can let the relationship they have with their children slip down on their list of priorities. Mothers can sometimes become distracted because the children's needs are often silently or softly present while demands from the outside can be unrelenting. And when a mother makes a decision about which of these demands she will respond to, it is usually the outside ones which result in a tangible form of appreciation.

A mother needs to examine the amount of energy that she expends doing for others outside of the family. If she finds herself wanting to be all things to all people, having difficulty saying no when asked to do something, or taking care of everyone but herself (and maybe her family), she might want to do some reading on the subjects of "people-pleasing" and "caretaking." One suggestion is *Codependent No More,* a book by Melody Beattie.

On the other hand, this issue of never being home could raise its head because sometimes teenage girls have a tendency to generalize a "sometimes" problem into an "always" problem. Perhaps mom has had an unusually demanding couple of weeks, or for some reason has been tied up more evenings and weekends than normal lately, and this is really the exception rather than the rule. If this is the case, mom can sit down and talk with her daughter to let her know that there is light at the end of the tunnel and ask her to bear with the hectic schedule for a short time.

Daughters should definitely let their mothers know when they feel that mom isn't around when she's needed. One reason to do this is that mom may turn out to be *very* surprised to know that she is still needed from time to time and that her daughter notices when she isn't home.

Another reason to make sure feelings are known is that while all of us, young or old, would like to believe that those who love us should be able to read our minds, the truth is they can't. Believe me—I've learned this the hard way. We are all responsible for expressing our needs in each of our relationships, be they mother/daughter, wife/husband, boyfriend/girlfriend, brother/sister, friend/friend or any other. Only after we let the person know what we need do we have the right to be angry if they don't respond.

Mothers of teenage girls often feel very unsure of how much, and in what ways, their daughters need them. Daughters tend to want to do less and less with their mothers. Whereas in elementary and middle school they would have loved going to the movies together, shopping, or out to lunch, now they prefer doing these things with friends their own age. As a result, mothers may start to feel that their role is becoming less important, and may compensate by seeking other activities.

The truth, however, is that although mom's role becomes less visible, it is no less important. No, her daughter doesn't need her to tie her shoes, braid her hair, or listen to her prayers, but mom does need to be there in a way that forms an invisible safety net that her daughter knows will be there should she lose her grip and fall. A mother can create this kind of role by listening nonjudgmentally to what her daughter has to say and by encouraging her efforts to reach for new experiences and goals.

Time is a valuable commodity for the modern day woman. But time is precisely what her daughter needs now and again. How to know when to make herself available is the challenge for a mother.

When a daughter feels like she has to make an appointment to grab three minutes with her mother, it is time for a chat. She should tell mom as honestly as possible that she misses having her around and wishes she would be home more. She might even say she "needs her," because this is really what it is all about.

Mothers should listen and honestly look at what is going on. Is the daughter's feedback accurate? Is she out of the house most of the time? Has she been so distracted by other commitments that she has been unavailable to her family and herself?

A daughter should also try to understand that as she grows older, mom will need more outside interests of her own, too. It really wouldn't be fair for her to expect her mother to just hang around in the event that she is beckoned.

My observation is that as daughters become older, the time they spend with their mothers decreases, but the quality increases. I may have spent four hours a day caretaking for my three-year-old daughter, but my thirty minute conversations with Julie about God, men, life, goals, feelings, and relationships have a much more powerful impact on keeping us connected and helping her feel supported.

It is important for mothers and daughters to share their needs with each other. If a daughter needs time with her mother, she should tell her. If she needs space, she should say that, too. If Mom needs to participate in some extracurricular activities for her own personal growth, she should say so. If she needs to sit her daughter down and touch base with her because she is feeling like she is watching a movie rather than participating in the play, she should also say so. The truth is that we still need each other.

"My Mom Embarrasses Me"

"**W**hen is she going to wake up and realize that this is the 90s? It's great that she wants to be different, but sometimes it seems like she still lives in the Ice Age and uses *no* common sense in public. It drives me crazy.

"I just want to curl up and hide when we're in a public place. When I try to guide her just a little bit, she gets ticked off and looks at me like I'm some kind of a demon for daring to criticize her. She criticizes *me* all the time, but I know it's supposed to be constructive, so I don't get upset. But that's all *I'm* trying to do—be constructive.

"People stare at her and she's oblivious to it. So when I try and help by telling her, 'Mom, you're eating really fast—why don't you slow down?' or 'Mom, you're screaming, and I'm right next to you,' I'm only trying to help.

"With my friends it's even worse. It's like she thinks my friends are *her* friends, and she thinks she's being cool. Why can't she just be a mom? All my friends' mothers don't come off as being obnoxious, and that's how she ends up being. Why can't she just wear an apron and nod her head when someone talks to her?

"When I ask her why she acts so weird, she says she's being 'rad' or 'hip.' These expressions were around in the 60s, and they don't sound too cool coming from a mother's mouth. So I'm sorry if I hurt her feelings, but subtlety does not work with her. For that matter, bluntness doesn't work with her!"

A Mother's View

"She Makes Me Feel Unloved"

"W hat am I? A leper? I get the distinct impression that if she had her way, when her friends come over she'd gag me and lock me in a closet. It's an awful feeling to know that your daughter would make you disappear if she could—at least when her friends are present.

"She doesn't make me feel that way so much when we're alone. She's more relaxed and less critical. But sometimes she gets this attitude of being _my_ mother, criticizing my hair, weight, laugh, and walk. I get the feeling that the worst thing I can do around her friends is to be myself.

"When did she stop loving me? When I changed her diapers as a little baby she didn't seem to care how I wore my hair. When I leaned over the tub to give her a bath, she didn't seem to care how much I weighed. When I read her a story, she didn't seem to care if my laugh was a little loud. And when I ran after her on the playground, she didn't seem to care if I was a little knock kneed. But now it seems like everything about me bothers her. If they had a recycling bin for mothers, I'd be in really big trouble.

"I don't understand why she gets so irritated with me when I try to be nice to her friends. You'd think she'd want them to feel welcome in our home. But she accuses me of being too chummy when all I'm trying to do is to get to know them a little.

"I also don't understand why I'm supposed to be perfect all of a sudden. She sure isn't. It seems to me that anyone who could become disgusted with her mother for humming in a department store could use some self-improvement herself.

"I think I get the picture, though. All I have to do is put on a wig, a mask, tape my mouth shut, stand still, and never eat the rest of my life to qualify for her utmost devotion. Boy, it's great to be loved."

Acceptance

S ome daughters are more embarrassed by their mothers than others. However, almost every pre-teen or teenager has had more than one experience of wishing her parent would pretend she was just the chauffeur or the maid.

For most teens, this phase of being acutely embarrassed by a parent is short-lived. In many cases the fear is that mom will treat her daughter like a child in public even though the same behavior might be perfectly acceptable in private. A daughter might fear that mom will spontaneously take hold of her hand, or put her arm around her shoulder at a time when she is determined to establish the fact that she is no longer a baby. (The same behavior might become acceptable again a year or more later, when the teen feels more confident with being out of the child stage.)

If, however, a daughter continues to become tense and strained whenever she is in public with her mother, there is probably more than a passing stage involved. If she continually criticizes her mother and tries to make her into someone she's not, then there is a breakdown in the relationship between the two that should be addressed.

First of all, let me say that many mothers are guilty of being overly critical of their daughters. They constantly criticize their teens, trying to mold them into what they want them to be. Sometimes the image they would like their daughters to adopt is very much determined by what they think would most impress their friends, and they try to control their daughter's looks, dress, and behavior. They don't want to be embarrassed in front of their friends by their daughter walking into the living room with green hair, a see-through blouse, and a foul mouth.

What I've described may seem to some an extreme scenario, but it illustrates that *both mothers and daughters* need to take a hard look at their own behavior in terms of criticizing each other. A daughter certainly wouldn't like to be told to more or less hide in a closet if her mother was having dinner guests, and such a request doesn't make mom feel too great, either.

Accepting each other is a cornerstone of the mother/daughter relationship. If a daughter is doing something particularly embarrassing, mom should tell her *in private* how she feels. But mom should also take a hard look at exactly what it is that is embarrassing her. Is it really worth mentioning, or is it something that simply indicates her daughter is not a clone of her mother? Is the mother's self-esteem dependent on her daughter looking and behaving in a certain way?

Daughters should take the same inventory. Does mom have a really annoying habit that she needs to be aware of, or is the daughter unable to accept her mother for who she is? Is the daughter's self-esteem so fragile that she believes her mother must meet a certain standard in order for the daughter herself to be accepted by her friends? Being supercritical of mom can really be a symptom of the daughter's dissatisfaction with herself.

What reflection is it on the daughter if mom doesn't wear makeup or is overweight? Why should her friends care if her mother runs marathons or eats bonbons all day? Those kinds of extreme behaviors might indicate that the mother needs to be more concerned about her health, but they don't affect who the daughter is. Likewise, what is the true reflection on mom if her daughter has purple hair and three pierced earrings in one ear? Her appearance might simply indicate a current fad, or a need to experiment with her looks. It doesn't affect who her mother is.

If mom is intrusive when it comes to her daughter's friendships, this is a topic that must be brought up *diplomatically* by the daughter. Everybody needs to set acceptable boundaries in their lives—including teens. Boundaries draw lines of acceptable behavior for others when it comes to issues such as privacy, relationships, safety, and interaction with friends. For instance, it is healthy for children to knock on their parents' closed door before entering. It is also healthy for teens to expect the same behavior and for parents to respect the boundary. It is healthy for parents to set acceptable standards for tones of voice and verbal interaction with their teens, and it is healthy for teens to set similar standards with their friends. If a daughter joined her mother without asking every time mom had a friend over for a cup of tea, the mother would have to set a boundary. Likewise, if mom tries to join in the fun whenever her daughter has a friend over, the daughter would need to do the same. Hopefully, mom will be able to listen and accept this boundary as a healthy step toward independence, even though it might hurt her feelings initially.

Daughters should ask their mothers (in a nonjudgmental way) what they are trying to accomplish by being so chummy with their friends. Perhaps it is important for mom to make them feel welcome in the home. If this is the case, the daughter could suggest other, more acceptable ways to achieve the same goal. If mom feels a need to get to know the friends firsthand, perhaps the daughter can sit down and tell mom a little about her friends. That way mom might feel less threatened that her daugher is spending so much of her time with people who are complete strangers to her.

In a family, each person needs to feel accepted, regardless of what flaws they possess. That's what "unconditional love" is all about. It means that *no one* is perfect (not even mom), but our imperfections don't diminish who we are as individuals, and they don't make us less deserving of love.

A family can suppport each individual to become the best person he or she can be by giving gentle feedback on issues that *can be changed* and *are significant*. If a person happens to have a large birthmark on his or her face, don't keep telling that person how noticeable it is. It can't be made to disappear, and it doesn't have anything to do with who that person is. However, if someone has a habit of interrupting people when they speak, then someone who loves that person should bring it to his or her attention.

Talk gently and lovingly to each other. Listen gently and lovingly. Give each other space to be who you are.

"My Brother's Such a Brat"

"Tere are so many kids that swear their younger brothers and sisters are favored. Well, I honestly think that's true, at least in my case. Mom always pays more attention him.

"I can come home with straight A's and I get, 'Good job, Julie.' He can do the smallest thing or get grades half as good as mine and he gets money or a present. If he is going to be treated like he's so special, then why do I even try to do well? It doesn't get recognized.

"And he's so irresponsible. Usually when she asks me to do something, somewhere around the first time she asks I do it and do it well. If I don't, I get, 'How many times do I have to ask?' He may decide to do something the 19th or 20th time he's asked, and he gets 'thank you.'

"Why don't my parents care about the fact that their son is a slob? Does mom think I like bringing friends over and having a huge mess all over the house? It's embarrassing. He smells, he's dirty, and he embarrasses me. Then, when I ask him to pick something up or take a shower, I get, "You're not his mother." Great! Well, his real mother won't correct him or train him to pick up simple messes. If and when she does, he weasels his way out of it. Mom and dad are so blind to his laziness. Or maybe they just ignore it.

"Maybe they just do this because he's the baby. Well, sooner or later I'm out of here, and my chores will be left for him. At this rate, how much do they honestly think is going to be left undone? Even more than now, you can bet on that.

"I don't understand. If he's so special and they focus so much attention on him, why didn't they just have one child? Then that one would always be the baby and they wouldn't end up making another child feel inadequate to her *younger brother.*"

"I Feel Like a Referee"

"Why isn't there a mandatory course in high school on how to raise children? I'm at my wits' end! What I want are two children who love each other, look out for each other, and support each other. What I've got is The World Famous Battling Brother and Sister. Come one, come all! The fighting never stops, day or night!

"She accuses me of spoiling him. I don't think that's fair. He _is_ younger, and she criticizes him so much that I think there are times when I do feel sorry for him. It must be tough having _three_ parents who constantly tell him what to do. And there is no doubt that she wins the prize for the most bossy.

"I'd be happy if she'd treat him at least as well as the dog. Him she pretty much ignores, but at least she doesn't pick on him and nag him to death. I realize it's too much to ask for her to treat him as she would a friend. You know, talk to him in a civil tone, listen to what he has to say, and care a little about his feelings.

"Then there are times I worry if I am showing partiality. She is older, and that is a tough position in the family. I ask more of her than him, and the expectations are higher. The oldest has more responsibilities and has to forge the way, fighting for most privileges. But if she were the youngest, she'd be upset that he gets more privileges because *he* was older, and we treat him more like an adult than her. I don't think I can win this battle.

"I try very hard to be fair. I give her the privileges and freedom she has proven she deserves—that's one of the few payoffs of being the oldest. I probably do go overboard in allowing him to learn responsibility and neatness at his own pace. But that's one of the payoffs of being the youngest. I think she hasn't really looked at what it's like to be the "little" one, with everyone else telling you what to do, how to do it, and when it should be done. Or what it feels like to have an older sister who gets good grades, is popular, and for whom most things seem to be a breeze.

"What I want is for them both to grow into happy, responsible, caring adults. But more than anything I want them to love each other."

Family Feud

I f there is more than one child in a family, the likelihood is that there will be some conflict between them. This is not necessarily bad, as it can teach brothers and sisters how to work out problems and compromise. But it can be very upsetting when they can't seem to be in the same room together without a fight ensuing.

Growing up with a brother or sister presents the opportunity to learn several valuable lessons: how to share, how to resolve disagreements, how to cooperate, how to care for someone who shares a big part of your life, and how to treat someone you care about.

Parents have a responsibility to teach these behaviors to their children, and can use the interaction between siblings as an effective teaching tool. Parents can't sit back and watch an older child bully a younger one: always taking what he or she wants, hitting the smaller one, or always having it his or her way. Allowing this would teach both of them that one should take what one can get in this world and not bother to consider the other person. The result would be self-centered behavior.

At the same time, mothers can't allow themselves to be so protective of a younger child that an older one feels persecuted. There may be a tendency to ask the older child to do for the younger one what he is quite capable of doing for himself. Mothers may also be inclined to make excuses for why the expectations for the younger one are different. Overprotecting the younger child can foster resentment between siblings, and that certainly doesn't help anyone.

Each child is unique. Mothers need to throw out the old premise, "treat everyone the same," which only results in no one feeling special. *Each* child is special in his or her own way. Their personalities are affected by birth order, their sex, genes, and how others relate to them as individuals.

If, for instance, the oldest daughter is an overachiever, she may need to be encouraged by the mother to lighten up a little and relax the high expectations she places on herself. If, on the other hand, a younger child is irresponsible and immature, Mom needs to set firm consequences *consistently* to teach him or her the values of responsibility and to follow through with goals.

Yet even as they try to treat their children as individuals, parents will leave themselves open to being accused of not treating each of them the same. The teenage daughter may be angry because she has to do the dishes, while the youngest one is angry because he can't stay up as late as his sister. When this happens, it is important for parents to remind their children that they respect their individuality, and try to treat them fairly, yet not exactly the same.

Mothers need to set certain boundaries in how brothers and sisters relate to each other. For instance, it should *never* be acceptable for one to hit the other. Someone is always at a disadvantage in a physical confrontation, and there are better ways to solve problems. If brothers and sisters are allowed to hit each other, they will come to believe that it is a generally acceptable behavior to hit and/or allow themselves to be hit.

Parents should also set boundaries on verbal exchanges. It is natural for siblings to argue from time to time, but it is not natural for them to degrade each other or speak in a voice meant to make the other feel humiliated. Name-calling using words such as "stupid" and "retarded" is off limits at our house. When the tone of voice gets out of hand, I ask my son and daughter to speak to each other at least as politely as they would an acquaintance at school.

Daughters need to take a hard look at how they treat their younger brother or sister. Are they extending the same courtesy they would to a friend or classmate? A family member deserves at least that much courtesy. If a daughter feels that mom is really being unfair by not placing reasonable expectations on a sibling, she should try to approach her about this situation rationally. She can explain what it feels like to be the oldest and why she fears the younger one is being spoiled.

Sometimes mothers should remind each individual that this is the only brother and/or sister they will have in the world. It is a special relationship, and should be treated as such.

"My Mother Lied to Me"

"I trusted her. I thought she trusted me, too.

"She can't tell me that she didn't think it concerned me, or that it was none of my business. That's a crock, because it does concern me—otherwise I wouldn't be so upset. And she can't say it's no big deal, because if it wasn't, she would have told me the truth.

"How can she possibly expect me to be open, honest and trustworthy when she sat there and lied to my face? How could she do that? She tells me how important honesty and trust is in a good mother/daughter relationship, and the whole time she was doing exactly the opposite. Well, she should practice what she preaches.

"I feel like I'll never be able to trust her again. After all, how can I trust someone who sits there saying one thing and doing the exact opposite? It's like everything I have always felt sure of about her is wrong. Now I'm not sure what to believe.

"I guess I just can't understand how she could do it. I'm her child. She's taught me to hate lying. But she lied to me.

"I want to understand; I really do. I want to understand how someone I look up to and trust can let me down like this. What excuse can there be for a lie?"

"I Lied to Her"

"It didn't seem like such a big deal at the time. She asked me about something I wasn't particularly proud of so, instead of being honest, I told her an untruth...well I lied. Some things really aren't her business, but it would have been so much better to have just reminded her of that fact instead of lying to her. To be perfectly honest (a little late, I know), I really didn't think she'd find out the truth. But she did. Now here I find myself in a situation where I feel like a naughty child.

"My daughter reminded me that I have preached and preached to her about honesty. I told her that if she ever lied to me—including lying by omission—I would never trust her again. I preached that a relationship is built on trust, and no matter what has occurred, we each must be able to believe that the other will be honest, even if it means saying something the other doesn't want to hear. And here I am, having made the Big Mistake. I have always told her, and believed, that I would trust her until I had a reason not to. Now _she_ has a reason not to trust _me_.

"How do I fix this? I wish I could turn back the clock and change my response. It was stupid, impulsive, and dishonest. I don't like to think of myself as any of these things, but here I am, the living epitome of stupidity, impulsiveness, and dishonesty.

"I can't justify the lie. I can't minimize the impact on our relationship. If I can't be honest about little things, how is she supposed to trust me when it comes to the big ones? I can only apologize to her from the bottom of my heart and tell her how badly I wish I could take it back. Then I can ask her to forgive me and give me another chance. I think she'll forgive me, but trusting me again will take some time. I'm willing to wait and work for it."

Honesty—A Tie That Binds

H ere is a simple bit of guidance for parents on the topic of lying to children: *don't*. If, however, a mother finds herself having made this blunder with her daughter, she needs to admit it. Sometimes telling the truth is hard because parents are afraid to show their human side. Mothers are reluctant to let their daughters know that they have made mistakes or acted less than honorably. I believe that parents are sometimes hesitant about being honest when it comes to certain topics because of the mistaken belief that if their children think that they have never messed up, maybe it will keep the kids from messing up.

Honesty is crucial between mothers and daughters. It is important to remember, however, that being honest doesn't necessarily mean a mother must tell her daughter every detail of her life. It does mean being honest when she chooses not to tell her something. Honesty and boundaries can be maintained by responses such as, "That is a personal matter between Dad and I, and I don't feel that it would serve any purpose to discuss it with you. What is your reason for asking?" Daughters may not like the response, but moms are letting them know that it is proper to set boundaries for privacy. This is a valuable lesson.

Just as daughters don't need to know every detail of their mothers' lives, mothers don't need to know every detail of their daughters' lives either. It may, however, be difficult for both parties to accept this.

When mothers are consistently honest with their daughters, a sense of security is created in the relationship. When so much in a teenager's world is shaky and insecure, it's comforting to know that there is someone she can come to for the truth. The relationship will not exist without this trust. Being honest even applies to the times a mother has to tell her daughter something she really doesn't want to hear.

Mothers must be consistent in never lying to their daughters. If they do, they can be sure their daughters will find out, just like mothers usually do when daughters lie. And it takes so long to build trust back into a relationship once it has been broken.

A daughter needs to confront her mother if she suspects a lie. But then she needs to listen to what her mother has to say just as she would like to be listened to under the same circumstances. She should be honest about how it feels to be lied to, but try to forgive her parent. Holding grudges and resentments is painful for both parties, and adds nothing to the resolution of the problem.

It's O.K. to make mistakes. But it's even better for a mother to admit it when she does, because it teaches her daughter to accept her own fallibility. All of us, regardless of our age, make mistakes. What makes us mature is our ability to learn from them. I have not met a single individual who has escaped the state of being human. Daughters are human, too, and that means they make errors, experience failures, and have problems. It serves no purpose for parents to lie about their own imperfections. How else will daughters learn that they haven't failed as people when they experience problems, make mistakes, or fail at a task? Instead they will remember, at least subconsciously, *"Mom went through this. She was honest about it. She seemed o.k. with it. I must be o.k., too."*

On a personal note, I'll be honest and tell you that I was most tempted to lie to my daughter the day she asked me how old I was when I lost my virginity. Every ounce of my being wanted to say, "Ummmm, thirty-eight."

"My Mom Read My Diary"

"I can't believe she did this. She's supposed to be my Mom. How could she have such little respect for someone who respects her (or at least *did* respect her) so much? She just took it upon herself to walk in, snoop in something that specifically said KEEP OUT!, and read it anyway.

"I trusted her. Why should I want her to trust me—why should I care—if I can't even trust her not to read my diary. That book was a place for me to write *my private* thoughts. It doesn't concern her. She had no right, none whatsoever.

"I feel so violated—as if I can't even stand to look at her, knowing that she has such little respect for my things. She intruded someplace where she had no business being. If there is anything in that book that I really wanted her to know, I would have told her.

"I've always respected her privacy. You don't see me marching into her room, going through things that are private and sacred to her. My privacy is sacred to me and she took that away. It's as if she gave me a gift and then one day just scooped it up, put it in her pocket, and took it away, never to be seen again. It's not fair.

"She wants to be able to trust me, she wants me to be honest and open. How can I be when I can't even trust her not to go into things that are none of her business. How can I be honest and open with someone who doesn't really value the meaning of the things that are so important to me? This was cruel, unfair and just basically wrong. There is nothing she can say that will take away what she's done.

"But I still want to know—why did she do it? How could she do something this horrible to someone she 'loves?' If she suspected something or needed to know something, she could have asked. When she does something like this, it makes me trust her less and less, and want to open up to her less and less. She's supposed to set an example. What kind of an example is this?"

"I Really Blew It"

"I couldn't help myself. I didn't plan to seek out the location of her diary and read it. True, I've felt left out lately—like I really don't know what's going on in her life. The hours she spends away from the family is increasing all the time. Who are these people she spends her time with? I mean, I've met them, but you really can't tell what they're like when they step off the front porch. And what goes on when they're away from the house? I know what she tells me about how they spend their time, but there are so many pressures for kids to be accepted these days. I'm afraid that she'll get in some situation she won't know how to handle.

"Sometimes she seems like a stranger to me. She's growing up, I know, but having a part of her that I don't know really scares me.

"I was cleaning when I saw the diary, and I read it. I knew it was wrong the minute I unlatched the cover, but I couldn't seem to stop. I so needed to know.

"Now I've broken her trust in a way that scares me more than not knowing her friends, activities, or even who she is.

Now I've entered her world uninvited—a hostile presence who took it upon herself to take what she wanted despite the consequences.

"And the consequences are so severe. When I really think about why I read her diary, I know it was to try to get close to her world, one that I feel less and less a part of. What I have accomplished, however, is to damage the trust between us— the only real connection I had with her.

"It's a hard lesson to learn. Her trust in me was like a fragile thread. It's badly frayed and only I can reinforce it. I'll work to make it strong again, even though I know it will take a long time."

Dealing With Fear Openly

I f in a weak moment a mother oversteps boundaries of privacy with her daughter, she needs to be honest—first with herself, and then to her daughter about why she did it.

For most parents, an act of intrusion into the private world of letters, notes, mail, diaries, and phone calls is motivated by some element of fear. On the surface, parents may believe they are just being curious when they pry into secret places, but in most cases there is a deeper level at which resides a fear of their child growing up and all that means.

Parents are afraid that growing up may mean experimentation with alcohol, cigarettes, drugs, and sex, and may lead to addiction, pregnancy, AIDS, and other dangerous consequences. Mothers fear that the hidden thoughts of their daughters may reveal a person they don't know anymore. So they ask themselves: *Who is this person? What clues can be found to help solve the mystery?*

At this stage in their lives it is not uncommon for daughters to stop telling their mothers everything, and to begin to have secrets. Mothers become tempted to find answers to their questions by sleuthing around like Sherlock Holmes. "Where lie the secrets of the stranger in my house?"

However, none of these fears justify the intrusion. As we will discuss many times in this book, trust is crucial to any relationship. How would the mother feel if her teen picked the lock on her safe and stole her jewels? Picking through a daughter's private belongings and stealing her secrets is no different; her secrets are her jewels. She may choose to share these jewels with her mother, but not if the mother has violated her privacy.

It is much better for mothers to share their fears. These can be conveyed by saying, "You seem to be withdrawn from the family and I'm wondering what's going on," or to ask directly if they suspect something: "Are you experimenting with drugs?"

In some cases, a mother may sense that her daughter is getting into some real trouble, and despite the mother's best efforts, she won't confide in her about what's going on. This may be a time for drastic action, but parents can proceed without being dishonest about it: "I checked your room today because I have reason to believe you are experimenting with marijuana. Let's talk about what I found."

If the damage has been done and Mom has already intruded into her daughter's privacy, there is no going back. However, mom should sincerely apologize and express how important her daughter's trust is to her. She can commit to never snooping again and follow through. She can explain that parents aren't perfect and they do make mistakes and that reading her diary was a big mistake. Trust will rebuild over time.

Daughters can help the situation by trying to forgive. Just

as they aren't perfect and sometimes do things they are really sorry for, the same goes for parents. Daughters can try to put themselves in mom's shoes for a minute. If they had made a mistake, wouldn't they like another chance to show they had learned from it? Mom deserves that chance, too.

And mom, don't do it again.

───────── `"!"`

"My Sister Told Me
Not To Tell"

"I love my sister a lot, and if I had trusted *her* with something I would expect her to keep it private. But I don't know what to do.

"Why did she put this on me? She made me promise not to tell, but I'm scared that if I don't, someone will wind up hurt. And if I do tell, our relationship will never be the same. She'll never trust me again, not with *anything,* and I can't say I'd blame her. It's probably not my place to say anything to my parents, but if I don't, then who will?

"I consider her my best friend. I mean, she's my *sister.* We've lived together since I was born. We should always look out for each other and protect each other, but should that be true even when my gut feeling tells me it's wrong?

"What kind of person has she become? I watch her changing more and more every day, and at times I don't even think I recognize her. She's so different from what she used to be, but I still can't let her down or break this bond that we have. It would have been so easy for her to just not include me in any of this, but she trusted me, and I'm so afraid of what will happen if I break that trust.

"But then there's my mother. She wants to know what's going on, and I want to tell her. She *needs* to know. My sister surely won't tell her; I'm the only one who can, and she's the only one who can help her. And what if I *don't* tell her and she finds out later that I knew? She'll never trust my judgment again.

"How do you choose between your sister and your mom?"

_____ *A Mother's View*

"To Intrude or Not to Intrude"

"**S**omething is going on, but I'm not sure what. She seems to be holding some secret, but when I ask what's wrong, I get, 'Nothing.' I swear she even avoids me at times. What's going on?

"I think it may have something to do with her sister. I see them talking more than usual, and when I enter their 'space,' which seems to be increasing rapidly in size, there is suddenly dead silence.

"I don't know how much to press the issue. I'm glad to see that they're getting along, and it seems that they *are* supporting each other. These are things I have wished and prayed for. So, how much should I intrude? I don't want to interfere in what appears to be becoming a close relationship. Yet she seems troubled—like her sister has told her something really important, or really scary, and she doesn't know what to do with it.

"If she did tell her a secret, I guess that's good. I trust her judgment to help her sister out if she needs it and to give good advice. But some secrets are just too big for a fifteen-year-old girl to handle. It also feels weird to know that there are some secrets going on around this house that I don't know about. After all, I am the mom. I'm supposed to be the one they come to when they have problems, right?

"She's always come to me before (at least I think she has) when she needed help. Still, I feel she is really hesitating now.

"Should I offer to keep the secret if she lets me in on it? What if it's something I have to act on? I think she might be afraid to break her sister's trust by telling me. I can understand that, because she and I have both learned the importance of trust the hard way. But how can I help if I don't know what's going on?"

To Tell or Not to Tell

S ometimes parents can feel like outsiders in their own homes. If there are secrets between sisters, it oftentimes becomes apparent to mom and dad even though the children may not realize it.

All of a sudden the two are talking in a civilized manner to each other. There are mysterious meetings behind closed doors and an obvious watchfulness when parents are around. Conversations suddenly drop off, even when the dog walks into the room.

It's hard for mothers to tell when they should stay out of these situations and when they should get involved. The fact that sisters are sharing important personal information with each other is evidence of a close relationship. This is not an area where parents are welcome, or where they should necessarily intrude. This kind of private communication can be a sign that the two are becoming more independent in dealing with their problems and are practicing problem-solving skills.

However, it can also be a sign that one of them is in serious trouble. If they never seemed to have a kind word for each other before and suddenly a solid pact has been forged, it may be a sign that one of them is in need of some help or that something has gone amiss. If this is the case, a mother may need to at least volunteer her support in a non-threatening manner. If she senses that her daughter isn't sure what to do with whatever she knows, mom can say something like, "You seem troubled about something, but when I ask you what's wrong, you say 'nothing.' Suppose you give me the situation in general, without any names, and see if I can help you?"

Daughters who are given information with a top secret classification may do well to keep the secret. The difficulty comes into play when the secret involves a clear indication that her brother or sister may be getting into something that might harm him or her. It is one thing to squeal when a sister has told her that she broke mom's favorite tennis racket and is trying to save up money to buy her a new one before she notices—she's in a fix, but she's trying to get out of it. There would be no purpose in breaking this trust other than to get her into trouble.

It is another situation, however, when she hides the fact that her sister or brother is smoking marijuana with friends after school. Maybe her sibling told her after being caught in the act; maybe she suspected and asked; or maybe her sibling really fears he/she's in too deep and needs help to get out. In any of these cases, this kind of secret is burdensome for a teen to keep and have to deal with.

If a sister is told a secret about something that could potentially be harmful to her sibling or others, she is in a serious dilemma. Does she break the trust with her sibling, or does she take whatever steps necessary to protect him or her?

It may be that she feels she could give the assistance her brother or sister needs if she had the proper guidance. If so, she might ask someone (a parent, other relative, teacher, or friend of the family) about the situation in a general way. "Mom, if you knew someone who was smoking pot, how would you help them?" If mom presses to know who it is she's asking for, the daughter can say that someone she knows needs help. This is an evasive answer, but not a dishonest one, and it would be best for the mother not to pursue this question at all. That way, whatever advice is given can be applied by the daughter without breaking the trust. If, however, the mother's response doesn't seem to help the situation, the daughter will have to decide what is more important at this point—protecting the trust, or protecting her brother or sister.

She should first tell her sibling that she is very scared for him or her, and volunteer to accompany the brother or sister to their parents for help. The brother or sister wouldn't have to do it alone.

If the brother or sister refuses, a daughter might have to decide to take the consequences of breaking the trust, with the hope that in the long run he or she will understand why she did it and forgive her. She could feel secure in the knowledge that her motive was purely honorable.

If she has to tell, she could start by getting a commitment from the parents to listen and to promise that they will help with a solution instead of immediately imposing a punishment. She shouldn't try to get them to promise that they won't get mad or upset, however, because they may have no control over their feelings.

If mom is put in this situation, she should be particularly sensitive to how difficult breaking the trust is for her daughter. The mother needs to give her daughter a positive stroke for taking this risk and for trying to help. Words alone won't do—mom will have to treat the situation as delicately as she would if she had to tell someone she loves that they have a serious illness. How the mother deals with the information could have serious implications for her children's relationship.

A family is supposed to form a safety net when one of its members is falling. It isn't just there to shine brightly when everything is going perfectly. Family members will have problems from time to time—mom, dad, sisters, and brothers. Drawing on the love, support, and strength of the family can help all of us weather our toughest storms.

Changes in
the Family

"Why Do We Have to Move?"

"Just when I get settled, make new friends, and get involved in a bunch of activities, Mom wants me to just pick up everything and leave—move to a new place, a new school, with new people and a new lifestyle. Well, no. I can't do that. I can't just pick up and forget about everything here. I can't just start all over again in a new place trying to make new friends.

"I'm scared. What if I don't fit in? What if it takes me just as long to forget about my friends here as it took me to make them? What if it takes me forever to make new friends? I'm not a person who can just go out and say, 'Hi! My name is Julie and I'd like to be your friend.' It doesn't work that way. I'm not good at meeting people, and I don't *want* to meet new people. I'm happy where I am. I love my life, my school, my friends, this house. I don't want to leave, and I'm not ready to leave.

"I don't understand. Why do we have to move? Don't Mom and Dad even care about my feelings? Don't I have any say in this at all? Nobody even bothers to ask my opinion on this. I guess I'm only a teenager, I'll adjust, so my feelings don't count. Well, what if I don't adjust? Then what? What if I am utterly unhappy where we're going? Have they thought about that, or do they even care how this affects me?"

"Moving On"

"**N**othing is simple. You might think that moving into a new house would be a joyous occasion. After all, the house is bigger, the school system is better, and I will have to spend less time on the road when going to work. Sounded like a smart move to me. Until I told my daughter.

"She doesn't want to go. I can't believe it, but I should have guessed. She's been in this house for a long time and grown up with friends from this neighborhood. I can see how it would be hard for her to leave.

"But I'm trying to do what's best for the family. She needs a room of her own and I have fears regarding the drugs, alcohol, and violence in her current school. But now, instead of feeling like a hero who is saving her from harm, I feel like a persecutor.

"She is totally miserable about leaving, and I'm feeling guilty—even questioning the decision. She is in a stage where friends and social stability are more important to her than most other considerations. Are the tradeoffs worth it?

"But her goals are short-term, and I'm trying to look at

the long run. When push comes to shove, will she even remember these friends in ten years? Can I let desires which probably have no bearing on our future determine the decisions we make today?

"And yet if I don't, will she be able to forgive me? This, here and now, is her reality, not ten years from now.

"I'm happy about the change overall, but the thought of leaving this house saddens me, too. The memories that live between these four walls are some of the happiest in my life. She grew from an infant to teenager in this house. The Christmases and Birthdays of the past will always be tied to this place. It's hard to turn my back on that, not knowing what the new one holds in store.

"But I know our new house will hold what we bring to it. Life is full of some small 'letting gos' and some big ones. This is definitely a big one."

A Family Decision

I s it any wonder that moving from one house into another ranks as one of the most stressful times in life, holding its place right up there with divorce and the death of a family member? Moving changes every aspect of daily life except who our family members are (and it may cause us to temporarily wonder about that) and perhaps our employer.

Daily activities which have become almost routine have to be redefined and reprogrammed. The layout of the house changes, households items are put in new places, we have to adjust to how the temperature, water, and lights operate, get used to the appearance of the house and yard, the neighborhood, and learn the new shopping areas. (Being an army wife who moved on an average of every three years, one of the changes I remember dreading most was finding a new grocery store.)

Daughters and sons feel these stresses as well as others, particularly teenage girls whose identities can be largely determined by their social lives. Their fear that they won't fit in at their new neighborhood and school may be based in reality, at least for a short time.

Teenage girls develop small groups of friends for the purpose of establishing a sense of security at what is often a very insecure stage in their lives. When a new girl enters a school, teenage girls can become threatened that their friends might like the new girl better than them. The strategy used to keep this from occurring often involves purposefully excluding the new girl. For this reason, it can be very difficult for the new girl to be accepted right away. But in time, personalities override fears, and friends are made.

Still, changes that come about from a move can be as frightening to a teenage girl as being fired from a job can be for an adult. It is important for the mother to understand the anxiety that moving creates for her teenage daughter.

Moving is not a decision that occurs overnight. There is a great deal of planning that takes place, and it is very important for the entire family to be involved in the process. Having the whole family along when looking for new houses and at new schools makes everyone feel more a part of the decision and less a victim of it. Soliciting opinions and considering what each family member has to say will help individuals accept whatever decision is finally made, even if it isn't what one or more of them wanted. But parents should listen hard to what their children have to say.

Parents have the ultimate responsibility (for better or for worse) to decide what is the best for their families. It works that way because they're older, hopefully more mature, and definitely more experienced. If the final decision is not what the children want, parents can at least tell all of the pros and cons which were weighed, and explain why moving seems to be the best decision overall. If the parents did involve them in the process, they will know in their hearts that the decision is justified (even though it may be hard for them to admit it), and they will adjust.

During the transition, Mothers can support their daughters' need to keep in touch with old friends by inviting them over, if possible, so that their daughters don't feel completely isolated during the initial adjustment period. In time, they will make new friends and will begin to feel secure again.

Daughters should try to stay connected to the people who love them. This includes old friends, parents, and other family members. Letters can also help daughters feel connected, and writing can be very therapeutic. Although it is hard to be patient, they should try to remember that they won't be the "new girl" forever. Sooner or later, someone else will become the "new girl" and they will know they have adjusted. Perhaps they can then try to remember what it was like for them, and reach out to the new person.

Mothers can share their feelings of sadness about leaving the house, too. The daughter may be surprised to know that she is not the only one who is having to let go of something.

"My Parents Are Getting Divorced"

"**W**hy are they always fighting? It isn't fair. I don't care if a divorce is the right thing to do. *I* don't think it's the right thing to do. As a matter of fact, I think it's the dumbest thing on Earth.

"I want both my parents living here. Why can't we just have a normal family like everyone else, with a mother, a father, and a child all living together happily in one house? I don't want to go through a custody battle or worry about how I'm going to divide my time between my parents. I shouldn't have to divide my time. I should be able to be with my parents when we're all together.

"What did I do to deserve this? I swear, I didn't want this to happen. Sure, when my mom and dad were in the middle of one of their huge fights, I wished anything would happen to shut them up, but I didn't mean for them to give up on each other. Or me.

"Why do they want to give up? They are both refusing to

try to keep this family together. They can work it out; I know they can. Marriage and love are supposed to last forever, or so I thought. If I can't depend on that, what can I depend on? They should do it for me.

"If they don't, what is it going to be like for me living with a single parent? I'm scared. I want to have a normal life. Now my life is going to be anything but normal. I'm going to have to be different from everyone else. And what if whatever parent I decide to go with or *have* to go with decides at some point that they don't want me anymore? Or worse yet, what if that parent needs me so much that I'm all they have to depend on? I don't want any excess responsibilities. I want my life to be the way it was before any of this started."

A Mother's View

"I'm Getting a Divorce"

"Well, it's finally decided. My husband and I are getting a divorce. I don't know whether to be elated because it means the end of all the fighting, or scared because I have never been on my own. I've always thought of myself as married. I don't even know who I am, except a wife and mother. I'm definitely scared.

"But I'm also happy. I deserve to be happy, damn it, and I am definitely convinced that happiness is an impossibility for me in this marriage. I've tried, God knows, to make it work. We've been through so much together, and above all else, he is the father of my children. I believe he tried to make it work too, as best he could. There just didn't seem to be a way.

"I feel like a failure, though. I'm smart enough to know that no one is 100% wrong or right. Why couldn't I make it work? Now my daughter has to suffer the consequences. She has to have her love for her parents split in two, like Solomon and his sword, but this time he completes the task.

"I want her with me, that's a given. And I _am_ her mother,

so that should give me certain rights. A daughter needs a woman to teach her how to be a woman. I guess I'm not teaching her great things about marriage, though, am I?

"And I guess a daughter needs a father in her life. I just don't think our fighting was good for her, and that she'll be better off with a part-time dad than with full-time stress.

"I hate the thought of what this is going to do to her. She'll feel so torn between the two of us. And what if I remarry? How could I even ask her to accept another man in my life, or hers?

"Love was supposed to last forever. It's an empty feeling to have this belief crumble. How can I ever trust love again? How will I accept the fact that I just lost half of my life chasing a dream that turned out to be a mirage?

"Things will be tough financially, too. We've been used to two incomes. I'll either have to work another job, or we'll both have to do without certain items and activities. Single parenthood has got to be the pits for kids *and* adults.

"I'm mostly scared, though. Can I make it as a single parent? Can I handle loneliness? Maybe my only chance to build a good marriage has come and gone. I don't want to spend the rest of my life alone."

A Family Facing Divorce

C hildren (teens included) so much want to believe that everyone lives happily ever after. We all do. But one of the hardest realities a daughter may ever have to face is her parents' divorce. Maybe *other* families break up, maybe *other* parents don't love each other, but it is a traumatic experience when children must accept these things in their own families.

It is also painful for adults to confront some harsh realities of life: people make mistakes, people change, love doesn't solve all problems. When it becomes clear that a marriage isn't going to work, another burdensome fact of life must be confronted: we can't have everything we want. Accepting these realities is tough enough for parents, but then there is still the issue of feeling like a failure to be dealt with. And if these endeavors don't keep them emotionally occupied, grieving the lost relationship and lost years will also demand its share of attention. Parents naturally become absorbed in all of these feelings—and then they must think about their kids.

Telling a daughter that the marriage is over may be one of the hardest undertakings of a mother's life. Teens who are caught inbetween the stages of childhood and adulthood may unconsciously revert to the younger stage, in their attempts to deal with the situation. Even when they are aware of this, it is difficult to avoid. They will not want this divorce unless the situation has been so unpleasant that they have distanced themselves from it in order to survive. But even when a daughter is surrounded by violence and chronic arguing, the reality of her family splitting up can be still more frightening than living the daily horror.

If I could give advice to any parent who is facing divorce, it would be this: you'll need to step out of your pain, anger, and fear and put your children's needs right up there with yours. (And I know how simple this is to say, yet how brutally hard it is to accomplish.) This is not to say that anyone should stay in a strangulating marriage, but at the same time, parents can't use their children as pawns of revenge, control, or as surrogate spouses. Making children's needs a top priority means that mothers must accept the fact that the other parent has a right to a relationship with the child too, and as long as it's safe, her responsibility is to cooperate, and not sabotage. It means a mother must shut her mouth when she wants to tell her child about the hateful side of her spouse. It means she must support the visits her husband has with her daughter despite her fear of what her "ex" will say about her. People can be lousy spouses but good parents. The mother may, out of her pain, want to keep her daughter for herself. For both her daughter's and her own sake, she must not.

If I could give advice to any daughter whose parents are

divorcing, it would be to try and understand how difficult this time is for her parents. Feelings of anger, fear, abandonment, and guilt will tend to keep her focused on herself, and while it is crucial that she express these feelings, it will also be helpful if she realizes that her mother is experiencing just as much emotional pain as she is. The choices are for mother and daughter to isolate themselves and deal with their feelings separately, or for them to share their feelings honestly with each other, allowing their relationship to become stronger through the crisis.

After a divorce the teen will have times when the reality viciously hits home, and she may feel much resentment. She may want to blame her mother or chastise her for not trying hard enough, and if she does, the accusation will cut to the core.

I remember a particular year after my own divorce, when Julie was about seven. Every month or so she staged what I would call a type of wake. She would play a tape of very sad music, put her father's picture on the pillow of her bed, and sit opposite it with a scarf draped over her head—to me it appeared that she was praying to it. Years later she explained that it was a time to block out everything else and close her eyes and think about her dad. She would remember happy times they had together and she would try to relive those moments in her mind. At the time, however, witnessing this scene really hurt. I felt so guilty that I had caused her so much pain, and helpless that there was nothing I could do to change it. So I let her grieve and tried never to make her feel guilty for expressing her feelings of loss.

When mom can consider her situation rationally, she can remember that sometimes divorce *is* the best solution. It is not healthy for children to grow up witnessing their parents' destruction of each other. Playing the martyr role by "grinning and bearing it" does not model the kind of behavior she most likely wants her daughter to learn. One positive lesson our teenager can learn from a divorce is that even when mom makes big "mistakes" she doesn't have to suffer forever. When faced with impossible circumstances, it is o.k. to cut our losses and move on.

A daughter may need to be reassured, though—sometime for years to come. Mothers can voice their thoughts and feelings in the following ways: "Yes, I love you and you are important to me." "Yes, I want you to have a relationship with your father" (if that is appropriate and safe). "Yes, two people (or three or four) can still be a family."

There will be trying times ahead. Single parenthood could probably win the prize for presenting the largest number of adjustments and responsibilities to a single individual at one time. If the lines of communication are kept open, however, these new challenges need not interfere with mother/daughter relationships. Above all, mothers must let their daughters express their anger, fear, hurt, and disappointment, even though the words may cut like a knife.

Lastly, mothers and daughters need to try to work together to overcome financial and other obstacles. It's tough for anybody to do it alone.

"Why Did They Divorce?"

"Whatever happened to the kind of family they used to show on t.v., where the father walks in from a day at work and says, 'Hi, honey, I'm home,' and then the children run down to greet their dad and they all have dinner together? What made those t.v. kids so special? I don't understand what I did to deserve this lifestyle. It's so unfair.

"I want my mother and father under the same roof, in the same bed, so that when I'm excited about something I can share it with both of them without getting on the phone or writing a letter. And the absolute worst feeling in the world is to know that I can't do a single thing about it. I could cry and beg them to get married again, but it wouldn't do a bit of good. They don't care how I feel.

"God forbid they'd think about what it's like for their daughter to have to grow up *visiting* her dad. Our visits are such a drag. I always feel like he's a temporary father. He exists when it's time for a visit with him, but then the time comes for me to go home and he's not involved anymore. I hate it.

"Why did they ever have to get divorced in the first place? Things would have been so much better if we had all stayed together. I dread growing up without a normal family. Maybe it's selfish, but I don't care. I want to be like everyone else. And why don't *they* care? Why doesn't it matter to them whether their child is happy or not? *I* care if *they're* happy, and I'm their daughter. They're supposed to watch over me together, to protect me from the world. How can they do this when they're not even under the same roof?"

A Mother's View

"So Many Losses"

"I wonder when she'll stop being angry with me. I thought we pretty much went over everything before the divorce became reality, but now that it's final, it's like we never discussed it.

"I thought she understood why things didn't work out between her dad and me, and that she accepted that our divorce was the best possible decision. But maybe I was just hearing what I wanted to hear, seeing what I wanted to see.

"I wonder when I'll stop feeling guilty. After all, _I_ didn't want life to turn out this way either. As a bride, my dream was to have a perfect marriage. I wanted to 'love, honor, and cherish, until death do us part.' I wanted to create a family with children who would wait with me at the door for dad to come home; he would kiss me first and then each of the children. I wanted to marry the man who would share my entire life and who would be there with me as I grew old. And we would have shared so much, it would all be all right.

"I don't know how to make it better for my daughter. She's got to feel as disappointed as I do that things didn't work out the way they were supposed to. ('Disappointed' doesn't seem to be the right word. Maybe 'devastated' would be closer to reality.)

"I love her so much. She is one of the few stable things I have left in my life. 'Stable' isn't the the right word to describe her place in my life either; maybe 'explosive,' but definitely 'fragile.' If I were to lose her, too, in all of this, I really don't think there would be much left for me to value.

"Our lives have been turned topsy-turvy. All the preparation in the world, all the talking, planning, and listening couldn't have prepared either of us for how it really is. My hope is that we can support each other through the tough parts.

"There are times when it's not so bad. There are even times when the space and independence I have created for myself feel good. But when she is feeling the pain so acutely, it overshadows any of the positives.

"I hope she'll forgive me and understand someday. For now, I understand what she's feeling, and I just wish I could make it better."

Reality Sets In

All the planning in the world can't really prepare anyone for what divorce is actually like. A teenager may have had all the whys and wherefores explained to her; she may have been given opportunities to express disappointment and anger over her parents' decision to divorce; she might have been warned that it would be tough. Still, being there and feeling the loss is not something that one can avoid, even by the best attempts at preparation.

Mom probably knew it would be hard, too. She knew there would be many physical, emotional, and financial changes. Perhaps she had weighed all of these adjustments against the option of staying together and knew in her heart that the decision to divorce was the right one. But at this point it really doesn't matter how right the decision was. Disappointment, grief, and guilt are not eradicated by a magic wand labeled "right decision." For instance, if you were told that your leg had to be cut off because there was gangrene and you would die otherwise, the right decision would be to have it amputated. But losing the leg would still definitely hurt, physically and emotionally.

Despite how difficult the reality of being divorced may be for the mother to accept, she usually has the advantage of feeling somewhat more empowered than her daughter. The chances are that regardless of who initiated the divorce, mom at least had some part to play in the final decision. This is not the case with her daughter—the divorce is something that was done *to* her. There was nothing she could do to stop it, which brings about a very helpless feeling. And it may be very hard for her to accept the fact that there is nothing she can do to change the situation she now finds herself in.

This is a difficult lesson for anyone to learn, yet it is a reality of life. There *are* circumstances in life over which we have no control. Divorce brings this point home to the teenager like an arrow finding its target.

When anyone is in a lot of pain, it is hard for that person to consider other people—it's like being wrapped in a shroud from head to toe and not being able to fully observe and respond to other people. One thing, however, which may help mothers and daughters survive this crisis, is for each to remember that they are not the only one who has suffered a loss. Moms need to realize amidst their pain that there is someone else who is suffering, and daughters need to do the same.

Getting out of the hurt long enough to consider what her mother must be feeling will help a daughter work through some of her anger and need to place blame. Mom has also suffered a loss—even if she initiated the divorce, it's a loss. It might help a daughter to understand what her mom is going through if she imagines what it would feel like to be the one who has to make the decision to have the family dog put to sleep because he is sick and in pain. Although you are the one who makes the decision, the grief you feel is not diminished. In fact, you may hurt even more.

Listening to her daughter vent her feelings is something a mother has to unselfishly endure, even though it may rekindle every ounce of guilt in her being. And mothers have to be honest with their daughters about how *they* are feeling as well. Sharing feelings will keep both parties connected during this trying time.

Most likely, the daughter held onto some tiny hope until the last moment, when the break was finally completed. She may have thought, *maybe once they are apart, they'll realize how much they love and miss each other and then they'll work everything out.* A daughter has to learn to let go of this hope. Thoughts like, *maybe when dad comes to pick me up and sees mom, they'll see each other differently; maybe they'll decide they hate living apart* are understandable. But at some point, holding onto false dreams will only keep a daughter from healing. She has to stop blaming and start adjusting because it is the only way to move on, the only way to heal.

If you lost your leg and spent all of your energy blaming the doctor, or blaming the disease that caused the amputation, you would be helpless to overcome the setback. Your energy would need to be refocused into learning to walk with crutches, or with an artificial limb. What's better—lying on a bed, angry and immobile, or learning new ways to move around?

Mom must empathize with her daughter's loss, and a daughter must empathize with her mother's. Then both can heal and move on. And there will be lessons learned from surviving the experience.

"I Hate My Stepdad"

"God forbid anything in this house would be easy. Everything has to be so impossible. If my mom had never gotten divorced in the first place, I wouldn't be having this problem.

"My stepdad is *so* unreasonable. He tries to take the place of my *real* father. He can never be a father to me. I hate him.

"He wonders why I never do anything for him. Well, he never does anything for me. We never get along, and even when I'm not doing anything, he comes up with something I've done wrong.

"Nothing is ever good enough for him. I can't be perfect *all* the time. If my grade point average is a 3.5, he wants to know why it isn't a 4.0. If I make a little mistake, he harps on it and overlooks anything good. He always tells me that everything is give and take, but he hasn't given me a single thing.

"When we do sit down and try to discuss things...well, this is really interesting. First of all, he's always right. My side never matters, and he couldn't care less about my feelings. *On anything!*

"When I do get to say something, he jumps to conclusions instead of *listening* (not just hearing) the whole story. If he is trying to explain something to me and I ask for a reason, the answer is, 'Go to bed' or 'Because I'm the parent.' Those aren't answers. Also, he always uses examples, like 'so and so gets good grades,' but when *I* bring up an example, he doesn't care about other people's children. He only uses others to compare me to when it works for him.

"He doesn't understand or even try to see that I am a human being and I make mistakes. I don't expect *him* to be perfect, and yet he seems to think I should be flawless all the time. Sometimes I need to make mistakes to learn, or just to make them. It's part of growing up, which is what I'm doing.

"His unwillingness to trust me with big responsibilities is crazy. If he doesn't give me a chance, how am I supposed to earn that trust, let alone keep it? Trust is part of good relationships. If he really wants a good relationship with me, and he says he does, why isn't he willing to make any changes or discuss anything?"

_____ *A Mother's View*

"Caught in the Middle"

"I wish there was a magic wand to make two people love each other. I love my daughter and I love my husband, but the two of them can't seem to stand each other.

"When I decided to remarry, my hope was that we could have a whole family again—I was a single parent for so long. I fantasized that my husband would gently find his way into my daughter's heart, and that she would quietly steal her way into his. I dreamed how he would become a man in her life who, although he would never replace her father, would be someone whom she could look up to and depend on for male support. I prayed my husband would come to see the special person she is and love her for it. Instead, as the conflicts grow and the communication stops, their hearts have closed to each other.

"I feel so much in the middle. Sometimes when he is harsh with her, I want to shake him and ask him who he thinks he is. And sometimes when she displays her hateful attitude toward him, I want to shake her and ask her why she is trying to hurt me. Both situations stab at my heart. When you love two people who just can't seem to even be polite, it's like being strung up between two poles. If you try to reach in one direction, it hurts the other arm. You're just stuck in the middle, unable to move.

"Sometimes I just want to run out of the house when they start fighting. (Maybe if I did and locked the two of them in the house alone, they might be able to work out their differences.) I am constantly playing the mediator, but I don't seem to be helping at all. They know how important it is to me that they get along, and neither seems to be trying nearly as hard as I am to make that happen. Yes, running away can seem very appealing at times.

"Maybe I was wrong to bring another man into the house. But I fell in love with him. That doesn't diminish how much I love my daughter. That love is different, and there's plenty of room in my heart for both. I just wish they had room in their hearts for each other."

Keep Them Talking

More often than not, a stepparent and a teenager are like oil and water. When mother and daughter are faced with this challenge, communication is extremely important.

A teenage daughter will probably have very strong feelings about the divorce, the new man, and the new marriage. She may feel she has already lost her father, and she has indeed lost her family as it always had been. Now mom wants to bring someone into the home who may, in her eyes, take her mother away from her as well. The daughter will more than likely be protective of her father's position and resistant to letting anyone even *think* of taking on that role.

It is helpful for daughters to express their feelings. They may be completely out of touch with the fear and only aware of anger, hatred, and resentment. They need to accept that fear of losing their mother may be at the base of their negative feelings toward the stepfather. It seems so much safer to cover fear with behavior that keeps others from getting too close instead of bringing it out into the open. Daughters also should examine the possibility that they may be taking out their anger over the divorce on this newcomer.

A mother needs to understand what may lie beneath her daughter's resistance to the stepfather, and to talk to her spouse about it. Discussing these issues can help prepare him for the tough work ahead, and may help him to take the daughter's behavior less personally. It would be wise to suggest that he try to relieve some of the daughter's concerns right up front by telling her that he knows he never could take the place of her father. He should try to explain that he understands that the father/daughter relationship is unique, and he knows she will only have that relationship with her own father. What he can be in her life is a man who has one very important thing in common with her: they both love her mother very much. A daughter may need to hear that he plans to support *both* she and her mother as much as he possibly can. Of course, this will be meaningless if he doesn't follow up accordingly.

For their part, daughters need to work hard to keep their anger over the divorce as separate as possible from their treatment of the new man. When legitimate conflicts arise, they should be discussed, preferably with the stepfather himself.

Mom must listen when her daughter tells her of problems in the relationship with the stepfather, and encourage her to express these directly to her husband. The conflicts may be hard to hear about, because mom wants the relationship between her husband and daughter to be good, but it is natural for problems to arise. They need to be resolved.

The preparation for the new household situation is very important. Mothers can't choose a man based on their teenager's likes and dislikes, but they can take into consideration what their daughter has to say about him before they remarry. Listening is crucial, despite the fact that the daughter may seem stubborn. Mom may be tempted to shut her out because she is not cooperating in her fantasy that everyone is going to live happily ever after, even when her daughter refuses to do so much as make eye contact with him when he talks to her.

Hard as it is to accept, mom must face the fact that she can't make a relationship happen between daughter and husband—she can't make them love each other. They each have to do their part. Acting as the perennial mediator will result in her hurting her relationship with her husband, her daughter, or both. When the daughter complains about her stepdad, mom should send her to him. When he complains about her, mom should send him to her daughter. Then they can talk about their differences.

Communicating is the only way to resolve the discord. A daughter who takes a risk by trying to work out the conflicts is one who is willing to see the benefits of family stability, and the same goes for the stepfather. If either individual's efforts don't work out, that person can at least say he or she honestly tried. Meanwhile, mom can let them both know what it feels like to be in the middle, and to have two people you very much love despise each other.

Maybe simply knowing their behavior hurts mom will help motivate them to get on with resolving their differences.

"My Mom Is Sick"

"How could this have happened? It was just a short time ago that she was so healthy. I remember like it was yesterday. And now look at her. I don't understand. Why did this have to happen to her? What if she won't be here to see me graduate or get married or have children? It isn't fair. Why did God pick her? She never did anything wrong, and we need her. It is so hard to watch someone you love go through all this pain, especially when she doesn't deserve it.

"I feel so helpless, like I am no good to her. There is nothing I can do to make her pain go away or to even make it easier. I can't even take away all the things that have happened between us. Nothing I have done or have said can be taken back. It's too late. I feel so guilty for the troubles we have had over the past couple of years, and there is nothing I can do about it. She must hate me so much. God knows I deserve it. I wouldn't be surprised if she dies hating me. I just wonder if there is time to make it better, or if that is even possible. It's so horrible to think that it takes something as awful as this to make us realize just how much we care about each other.

"Why? That's the only question I have. Why? Why did this happen to her of all people. I don't know how to handle this. Should I be angry at God for doing this to us or should I be turning to Him for love and support? I know it isn't right, but I feel like he's responsible for what is happening to her. So why do bad things have to happen to innocent people, especially people I love? How am I supposed to act or to feel?

"The worst thing is that everyone expects something different from me. Everyone tells me how to act, what to do. No one thinks about my feelings. Do people think this is easy for me? My entire future may be changed and people still expect so much from me. I can't give everyone everything."

"This Wasn't Supposed to Happen to Me"

"**I**'m sick, and I can't believe it. I thought I was invincible. Everyone _else_ gets sick, and I take care of them. That's the way it's supposed to be. But here I am, faced with an illness I thought only happened to others.

"I'm angry. I've been a good person, damn it. I've tried to be a good wife and mother. I think I have been. Now family life has to go on without me. Life itself has to go on without me, because I'm too sick to participate. What the hell did I do to deserve this? I can't even go to my daughter's concerts and games.

"I'm weak. I can't even manage to get through the basic activities of the day—eating, bathing, dressing, conversing, without feeling exhausted.

"I'm depressed. I can't hold a normal conversation with anyone. We are either talking about my illness (which I am sick to death of thinking about) or I'm too preoccupied with my illness to really care what they have to say. Food is tasteless. Colors are dull. The sunlight seems so far away.

"I feel guilty. My family needs me, but I can't care for them. They are having to pick up all the slack—cooking, cleaning, laundry. I can't be the mother my daughter wants and needs at this point in her life. She shouldn't have to be worrying about me. She should be enjoying life, being troubled only by relatively simple problems like boys and school. But I see the sadness and concern in her eyes, even when she tries hard to be in good spirits. I try to keep a stiff upper lip for her, but I know she sees the same in my eyes.

"I'm scared. What if I don't get better? What if I can never participate in life any more than I can now? Or worse yet, what if I don't survive this illness? There's so much ahead I don't want to miss—college, weddings, grandchildren, watching my daughter make a life of her own and having her share a small corner of it with me.

"God, help me get through this. Help all of us get through this."

Coping with Serious Illness

W e are often reminded that life isn't always fair. But if fairness is defined as not having problems if we're "good," then life is *never* fair. The fact is that all human beings, regardless of their behavior, have problems and face crises. More often than not, there does not appear to be rhyme or reason to this reality. However, most of us have a need to try and make sense out of this apparent injustice.

Rabbi Harold Kushner wrote a book entitled *When Bad Things Happen To Good People*. The first premise that F. Scott Peck undertakes in his book, *The Road Less Traveled*, is that "Life is difficult." It appears that none of us can expect that if we make all the right decisions and live loving, godly lives that we can be guaranteed a life free from problems. Or from illness.

Serious illness can occur in any family at any time and create a major stressor, particularly when the mother is the one who becomes ill. Despite Women's Lib and the fact that most women work outside of the home, in most families the mother continues to be the heart of family life. She is the center, the hub around which all other family members and activities revolve. When she is out of commission due to illness, emotional stress forms within each family member; each must deal with the fear of losing her, the anger of being abandoned, and the guilt of somehow being responsible for her illness.

The stress can be so severe that a conscious effort oftentimes must be made if the family is to continue to work together. Unfortunately, the tendency is for each family member to go off and hide in his or her separate corner to lick their wounds. The only way the emotional stress can be dealt with (and perhaps even used to hold the family together more tightly) is by encouraging each other to express feelings and to offer support as they do so. Negative feelings as well as positive feelings can keep a family emotionally connected if they are shared in a supportive environment.

Husbands may try to become the mother to the children. This is understandable to some extent, as they will need to pick up additional responsibilities. At the same time, however, a husband and father may be short on patience and not willing to honestly discuss the nature and extent of the mother's illness with the rest of the family. He may also be so exhausted that he doesn't have much energy left with which to give emotional support to the children. Emotional stress can be as draining as running a marathon.

In this situation, daughters most often feel frightened. Even though their relationship with mom has likely had its share of ups and downs over the last few years, this is the only mother the daughter will ever have. Even though it may be hard to believe at times, it is and will continue to be one of the most important relationships in her life.

Despite the actual seriousness of the illness, the daughter may fear that her mother will die, and this translates as her mother leaving her. But she needs her mom, and therefore mom just can't leave. Sometimes this fear will be expressed as anger, where the daughter may become easily enraged. The feelings can be all mixed up where she may feel angry at times when asked to help out more, but then she will feel guilty for being angry. For instance, she may chastise herself for being so self-centered as to become angry when she is asked to get off the phone and cook dinner. She may also feel guilty when she goes out and has a good time, because her mother is sick at home.

But the daughter cannot change the nature of the illness. She needs to keep this fact in mind, and mom may have to be the one to remind her. The mother can explain that while she knows how upset the daughter is that she is sick, it is important for her to remember that she is very young and must still have a life. Yes, she will be asked to help out more, but the best gift she could give her mother would be to laugh and have fun when the opportunity presents itself. Mom can explain how guilty she feels for bringing sadness to her daughter's life, and how happy it makes her to see her daughter smile. (A daughter often feels she needs permission to do this.) Daughters can help the situation by offering to help out more and by finding someone with whom they can safely discuss the feelings of fear, anger, and guilt.

If mom is feeling resentful that life is going on without her, that's normal, and doesn't make her a bad person. But she must find some way to deal with the resentment other than by putting a guilt trip on her daughter or on other family members. Depending on the seriousness of the illness, personal and family counseling may be needed to help the family deal with the emotional stress.

The daughter needs to be assured that she will be fully informed about changes in the illness. If information is held back, she'll know it, and her imagination will be her worst enemy. She should be given the facts as they occur, so that she can make sense out of what she sees. Honesty will allow her to cope with what is happening much more effectively.

Self-Image

“Who Am I?”

“There is something that I'm so confused about. Okay, I know this sounds really stupid, but I feel like I don't know who I am. I am at the point where it seems like I know *nothing* about myself—how I feel about anything, what's important to me, or what I want out of life. I should know myself better than anyone else should know me, right? Isn't that what people always say? Well, why is it that I don't?

“Sometimes it seems like I don't understand anything about myself anymore. If someone was to ask me a question about what I would do in a certain situation, I honestly wouldn't know what to say.

“I don't feel like my own person. I just go through life, day by day, playing roles and pretending for people to make *them* happy, but never deciding what I want myself. I bet if someone were to ask someone I know, ‘What is she like?’ that person would sum me up in one word: *fake*. They'd probably say I'm not sincere or together about anything! And that is so true. I don't understand how I am expected to be happy and have friends and all that when I don't even have a real personality.

"It seems like so many people go through life with a specific goal, knowing exactly from the start where they are going, and they follow through and get exactly what they want out of life. I don't even know what I want, much less how to go about getting it. I don't know what kind of person I want to be, how I want to spend my life, who I want to spend it with, or anything. And I feel like I never will know at this rate.

"For instance, how do I want to make a living? Should I go to college? Do I want to get married? If so, to what kind of man? Will I ever find him, and if I do, will the marriage last? Do I want children? So many questions. What I really don't understand is how to get the answers."

"The Stranger in My House"

"Who is this person I call my daughter? Sometimes I haven't the foggiest idea. Sometimes she seems to change almost every day, often becoming the complete opposite of who she was the day before.

"Yesterday she treated her brother like a despicable gnome; today she made him breakfast. Last week she wanted to go to college, this week she wants to be a waitress. This morning her goal was marriage and a house full of kids. Now it's evening and she doesn't feel marriage is a 'worthwhile institution.'

"I don't know why I let myself get sucked into concerning myself with her beliefs or goals of the moment. Sometimes I get so angry when her values have suddenly switched to something totally foreign to what we've tried to teach her. Then I might be relieved to learn she is making some sound, mature plans, only to be let down when she changes them the next week.

"Sometimes I wonder if she says some of the things she

does just to get a reaction out of me. Well, I seldom disappoint her. It seems like as soon as I begin to relax with who she is this week, she does an about-face and becomes someone else.

"If I could make some sense out of the changes, maybe it would help. I mean, if her attitudes, beliefs and goals were progressively going down the tube or evolving into an increasing sense of maturity and responsibility, maybe I could adjust better. At least I'd know in what direction she was going. But no, it's left one day, right the next, then maybe up, and then diagonal. It's sort of like her attitudes are a ball in a pinball machine. Unfortunately, I feel like the I'm the ball being bounced every which way and the person playing the game is a master.

"I guess she must be feeling the same way too, though. I really wish I could keep from reacting so much. I wish I could just listen and smile and say 'That's nice, dear.' It can't make it any easier on her for me to overreact each time she bounces a new idea in my direction."

Practice Makes Perfect

It is unsettling for parents to feel they don't know much about a member of their own family. It can be frightening for them to start to feel confident that they are beginning to recognize this person again, only to have her transform overnight for no apparent reason. It can be like having a daughter sitting at the dinner table one night and finding a werewolf sitting in her place at breakfast. And there wasn't even a full moon!

The teenage years are a bridge between childhood and adulthood. During this journey, beliefs, attitudes, and goals must be tested out for their worth and acceptability. Testing involves trying new tasks, risking new behaviors, trying on various personalities, and verbalizing the beginning buds of a personal philosophy.

Talking about what she wants and believes helps a teenage daughter in the development of who she becomes and what goals she sets for herself. This activity is like trying to find the beginning pitch of a song: you have to start by singing the first note. If it's too high or low, you can make an adjustment, but you won't know until you sing it. After you sing the note enough, it always comes out on pitch.

Daughters must try different pitches to see what song they want to sing, and what is their best key. For some, the key of G may be best; for others, perhaps the key of C.

A daughter must talk about her thoughts, feelings, and goals to see how they fit. She must try a song to see if it's right. Then she can throw it out if it's not, but she won't know before singing it.

Asking mothers to be the patient audience—to wait for the singer to get it right—is tough. The truth is that mom is a captive audience who can't leave the theatre. She may want to throw tomatoes at some selections, but the other possibility is that she may be frozen in awe at the beauty of the song.

If mothers can accept the fact that their daughters are finding their ways and experimenting with new ideas, they may be able to keep their sanity. Listening is important, regardless of how much a mom hates what she may be hearing. Her daughter may not yet be skilled at examining the pros and cons of new concepts, nor can the mother expect her to be. Daughters must practice, which means experimenting with all sorts of ideas. Mothers can given honest feedback when asked.

If mom can be patient, uncritical, and not get too attached to what she hears as her daughter practices at the time, she may be given the gift of watching the singer evolve from an ostrich to a nightingale.

Maybe the daughter will sing mom's favorite tune, maybe she won't. But simply because it will be her own melody, it will be beautiful. And mom can sing her own song to her daughter, too.

"I Have No Life"

"T.G.I.F.? Not quite! More like thank God it's Monday, because then I don't have to sit home by myself.

"It isn't fair. Everyone has their own group of friends that they spend *every single weekend* with, and I don't belong with anyone. Lately it seems like my idea of fun is to rent a video, order out, and sit in a chair watching t.v. until so late that I fall asleep. That might be o.k. once in a while, but every weekend it's completely boring! Then I go back to school on Monday and the few friends I have ask, 'What did you do this weekend?' And what do you think my answer is? Every single time I have to say, 'Oh, not much, pretty boring really.'

"At least if I had a boyfriend I could say that I don't have time to see my friends, but I don't have one. There is no excuse for why I have no life, except that maybe I'm just such an unapproachable geek that nobody cares to waste their precious time on me. What's the matter with me? God, I must really be awful to be around.

"Nobody else in the world has as boring a life as I do. I

mean, most people come home and talk on the phone all night, and maybe do their homework if they can fit it into their busy schedule. But not me. If I were to come home and pick up the phone, I wouldn't even know who to call.

"When Friday night comes, everybody calls their friends and they always do *something*. How come nobody calls me? Why can't they seem to fit me into their plans?

"My parents sometimes offer to let me go with them to the movies and such, but, no offense, I couldn't be caught dead with them on a Friday or Saturday night. I can see it now: me sitting there so cute between Mom and Dad while all the kids at school who are there *together* walk down the aisle, pointing their fingers at me and laughing. *No thanks.* I'd rather be bored at home than be the laughing stock of the school.

"There *has* to be something wrong with me for *no one* to include me in their fun."

"Her Biggest Fan"

"I don't know whether to kick her butt off the chair or try to hug away her misery. She just sits around, depressed, because she has no social life. It's really sad to see her spending so much time alone, but when I suggest we do something together, she refuses.

"I don't know why she won't pick up the phone and call someone. She's just waiting around, as if friends and social activities are going to drop from the sky right into her lap. When I suggest she call someone, she just snaps at me.

"She doesn't seem to want to be with the family and she doesn't want to be alone. I don't have any other choices to offer. I know I can't substitute for friends, but it seems like it would beat being miserable. Yet she's very cranky most of the time, to a point where I hesitate to even approach her.

"I'm trying to remember what it was like. It's hard, though. I seem to recall being alone a lot, but I don't remember how it felt. Selective memory, I guess.

"I don't understand why the phone isn't ringing off the

hook. She's attractive, enthusiastic, considerate, and usually a lot of fun. I know she must be doubting herself now because no one includes her in their plans. I know it bothers her that she doesn't have a boyfriend.

"I'd be willing to send out letters of reference to her friends, lauding her many qualities, but I know how embarassed she'd be. Maybe I'll just send her a letter of reference from *me,* reminding her of what a great person I think she is. I know it won't mean as much to her as it would coming from a friend, but it would be true, and from my heart."

Surviving the Dry Spell

When a teenager's social life slows down, two weeks can seem like an eternity. Being with other teens is a necessity because social activity is a kind of unspoken support system, a much-needed validation of existence.

In order to understand this idea, try to imagine a world where most, but not all, of the people were invisible. If you happened to be one of the few visible ones, you would definitely seek out the other visible people and form a group.

In many ways, teenagers are like a strain of unique beings roaming the earth. They are only teens for a few years, and there is a minority of people on the earth who are teens at the same time they are. And as we've discussed, teens have very unique characteristics. They need to be together, partly to convince each other that they aren't strange or peculiar, and also to find the reassurance of a group in which they belong.

When teenage girls go through a "dry spell," so to speak, where they seem to be out of the loop of activities, they tend to doubt themselves. They ask themselves, "What's wrong with me?" and "Why doesn't anyone like me?" They may not realize it, but what they are doing is assessing their self-worth by what they perceive others think about them.

Teens often have difficulty seeing the light at the end of the tunnel. It may be true that for a short period of time they haven't had much of a social life. However, teenage girls tend to project this dry spell as a permanent condition which will last for the rest of their lives.

Mothers should encourage their daughters to pick up the phone and initiate some activities themselves. Sometimes the daughter can get into a passive mode where she just waits and waits for something good to happen. It is important to teach daughters to take charge of their lives, and one way they can do this is by initiating some social contacts during the dry spell. Hopefully, the daughter won't fall into the trap of only pursuing the most popular girl in the class to be her friend. There are always many wonderful kids in a school and many who are a lot of fun to be with are often overlooked. A mother can encourage her daughter to think about friends (or potential friends) with whom she has something in common.

Daughters should try not to fall victim to situations where they are always waiting for someone to include them in what they are doing. They can pick up the phone and suggest going to the mall, the movies, or wherever. One of the hardest parts of a dry spell is the sitting around and waiting, but there is no reason why she needs to do this.

Mothers can encourage daughters to get out and have some fun. She can allow her daughter to have an overnight guest, or a slumber party. One piece of advice that I gave Julie (which she assured me was totally "off the wall") was to walk up to some new people and say, "Hi. My name is Julie." She guaranteed me that doing something like that was a sure way to get a reputation for being a dork. (O.k., I'll admit it: I was desperate at that particular point in time.)

Mothers can also support their daughters by inviting them to participate in activities they normally enjoy doing together. These activities might be shopping, going to a play, or attending some other event. When daughters are feeling rejected, they'll find their moms can really help if they'll let them.

"I Hate My Body"

"I hate my body! Why is it that guys only like girls if they have a big chest and perfect curves? I can't get any guy to like me because I have *no* body. I look like a toothpick. I feel like I'm never going to develop. Look at me. I have no hips, no chest, my stomach is fat, my butt's big, my legs are gross. There's not one thing attractive about my figure.

"I'm sick and tired of waiting around for my body to change. Every single girl at my school is bigger than me. I'm the only one left who has not developed yet. I can't even wear half the clothes I try on at stores because my body doesn't fill them out. And guys notice it too. Guys never look at me because of my mind or my personality. They only look at other girls because of their bodies, and I don't have one.

"Everything I wear or try to wear makes me look like I'm still in elementary school. Except for my height, I *could* still be in elementary school. I'm so embarrassed in the locker room when everyone else changes and has something to cover and I'm just standing there embarrassed because I'm

133

the only one who doesn't.

"Am I always going to look like a stick? Shouldn't I have started to develop by now? I mean, what's wrong with me? What if I never change? You can't tell the difference between me and a boy except by my face. Girls are supposed to change into women. Will I ever be a woman?"

_____ *A Mother's View*

"If She Could Only See"

"**I** feel so helpless when she feels this way. I want to speed up time to spare her the suffering but I don't want to lose a precious minute with her. I want to take the boys in her class and slap them into sensibility. I want to let her see herself through my eyes because she is so beautiful.

"I don't really know what to say. Is there a magic phrase? I've tried to tell her that she is far too critical of herself and that she is just how she is supposed to be at this point in her development. We don't change into women overnight, and it's normal for us to be in between for several years. But it doesn't seem to help. I want to tell her that she is so much more than boobs and hips, but I think it would sound trite. More than anything, I want to tell her that she is the most beautiful girl in the world, but I know she wouldn't believe me.

"The funny thing is, it's the truth. I've watched her from the beginning. First she was just a ball of baby fat with two eyes and a big mouth. Then she grew some hair and her form gained definition. I watched her learn to move her body, from clumsy crawling to grace on two legs. I watched her teeth come in, fall out, and come in again. Now she is slowly turning into a woman before my very eyes. To me it is like watching a miraculous transformation.

"Right now she holds all the promises of womanhood, pure and innocent of all there is yet to be. How could she be anything but beautiful?

"*Be patient, my love*, I want to tell her. *And try to look a little closer at all that you are. You have your whole life to become a woman.*"

Reassurance

At times like these, parents can feel pretty helpless, since there is nothing they can change. They can't make time speed up; they can't change genes which may account for the length of time it takes for their daughter to get through puberty; they can't change the cultural emphasis on physical attributes; and they can't staple shut the mouth of every kid who takes a pot shot at their child. So mothers can feel pretty inadequate as they go about trying to help their daughter through these feelings.

Moms can reassure their daughters that they will, without a doubt, grow up and have the necessary attributes, to one degree or another. But they need to point out that everyone is different, and some girls develop later than others. Mothers can also explain that as teenagers we tend to be more focused on body parts than at any other age, because the body parts are relatively new; and if everyone suddenly started growing antlers around age thirteen, teens would be checking out everyone's antlers.

Most parents can't believe it when I tell them what helps the most. I got this jewel of wisdom straight from Julie's mouth, or I wouldn't have believed it myself. What is *"crucial"* (as she puts it) is for me to make sure to tell her that I think she is beautiful. At first I found that hard to accept, because when I saw she was in one of those moods and I tried to tell her that I thought she was beautiful, she usually rolled her eyes and looked away. Then I realized that telling my daughter that she was beautiful *did* make a difference, and the reason is that a parent's opinion is still influential, and still gets through even when it may seem like it is being ignored. As we grow to adulthood, we are less dependent on our parents' opinions, but they never completely lose their importance to us.

In these moods of uncertainty, teens can feel very vulnerable, although this feeling may be covered with angry quips when a mother tries to help. But when the daughter is honest about what is really bothering her, it helps the mother offer support.

Although nothing can speed up time or change the process of development, mothers can offer a voice of hope in the night. They can be the consistent person in their daughter's life who sees them as beautiful and knows that they will without a doubt grow up, and everything will fall into place.

A Daughter's View ———————————— `"!"`

"How Could I Have Done That?"

"I am a horrible person. No wonder nothing good ever happens to me—I don't deserve anything good.

"How could I have done it? Of all the mistakes I could have made, I guess I just had to make the worst one. Anyone in their right mind would have stopped and seen what they were about to do was wrong. That is if they had even considered what they were doing in the first place. But not me. I feel like a heartless, horrible person who doesn't care about anybody but myself. How could I be anything else to go and do something so stupid and cruel? Where were my feelings?

"True, I feel guilty about it now, but a lot of good that does me, or anyone else. It's already over and done with. Now it's a little late to want to change things.

"It's no wonder nobody trusts me or wants to be around me. I know if I was someone else at school, I wouldn't want to hang around me either. As a matter of fact, I'd probably make it a point to avoid me. I show no respect for other people's feelings, so I obviously can't respect myself.

"How many girls do you know who can say this many horrible things about themselves and still be telling the honest to God truth?

"Sometimes I wish I could hurt myself as much as I've hurt other people with the stupid things I've done. I surely deserve to be hurt back this time, that's for sure.

"I don't know how I could ask to be forgiven. I really screwed up. But the thing is, I don't want to spend the rest of my life feeling guilty or bad. How do I forgive myself for something I know in my heart was about the cruelest thing I could have done?"

"I Know She's Not a Bad Person"

"She's feeling awful about what she did. I'm angry with her too, but she seems so upset that I don't think she needs me to tell her that. She has taken this mistake and completely condemned her character for it. Everybody makes mistakes, though.

"I won't have any trouble forgiving her, but I am wondering if she will be able to forgive herself. She is really a caring, thoughtful person, and this mistake doesn't change any of that. But she won't seem to let it go.

"I wonder if I have taught her to be so hard on herself. I know I have trouble forgiving myself when I make a mistake. I hate to admit it when I screw up, and when I'm forced to face it I get angry with myself.

"I wonder how unforgiving I have been toward her in the past. I know there are times I have gotten angry with her for what really boils down to being imperfect.

"But none of us are perfect. I know that. Sometimes it's hard to accept—I still can try to fool myself, like maybe if I try real hard, I *can* be perfect. But that would make me God, wouldn't it?

"At least she has accepted responsibility for her actions. I tried to point out that it is a strength to admit when we've done something wrong, and to not try to blame others. I'm just not sure I've really demonstrated that in my behavior though.

"She can learn from this mistake. *I've* learned that I have a lot of work to do to show her, and not just lecture her, that we're all only human beings. We'll make mistakes, and we need to accept them, learn, and move on.

"I know I love her, and this doesn't change that at all. I just need to make sure she knows it."

The State of Being Human

O ne of the biggest challenges of being a parent is teaching children to deal with the state that all of us are in—namely, the state of being human. By this I mean that no one, regardless of age, can really live a creative, productive, and loving life if they are in denial of who and what they are, which includes faults as well as virtues.

What we are is human. Who we are is an individual person, unique in the world. But being human and accepting what comes with it means that we realize we will make mistakes, have problems, and even fail at times. None of these situations makes us less of a person, but fighting this reality blocks us from learning, developing effective problem solving skills, and progressing as we go through our lives. We can get stuck with our anger at not being perfect, and refuse to forgive ourselves and others for not having reached that goal.

We can't come to love ourselves if we are in a perpetual state of self-blame. And if we don't love ourselves, our ability to love others will be significantly diminished. Also, if we can't forgive ourselves, we will have great difficulty forgiving others.

I bring up these points because daughters learn how to deal with their own imperfections from how their mothers deal with theirs. Mothers set the standard, and through their own behavior, model what is acceptable and not acceptable. Mothers communicate forgiveness or blame through their words and actions, and have a powerful effect on how daughters accept and learn from their own mistakes.

If a mother feels it is not o.k. to make a mistake, she will be angry with herself or perhaps be inclined to blame others. It takes a lot more energy to engage in self-criticism and to hold resentments than it does to forgive. Accepting and forgiving mistakes that have been made frees the individual to move on and learn. The alternative keeps the person stuck in the past by not being able to let go of it.

Many mothers need to take a look at themselves on this issue. There is much pressure nowadays to be a "Super Mom," to be all things to all people. Mothers need to ask themselves whether they expect this of themselves by examining how they handle their mistakes.

Mothers should feel free to talk to their daughters about their own mistakes. They can share the ones that they had to struggle to let go of, and ask their daughters what they might have done in the same situation.

Daughters need to remind themselves that everyone in the entire world has done something they regret. What separates the "men from the boys," or in this case, the "girls from the women," is whether or not they can learn from it. No one is born wise. Wisdom comes from a series of experiences out of which we accumulate new pieces of knowledge.

Making amends is one way that helps most people let go

and move on. That usually means taking the step of sincerely apologizing to those who have been hurt. This serves two important purposes: it helps the other person get over the injustice, and it frees us to move forward.

Mothers can affirm their love for their daughters and tell them that they do not expect them to be perfect. Then both parties should try to follow that up with forgiving attitudes toward themselves, each other, and any other friends, relatives, and acquaintances who may have been judged too harshly.

"I Didn't Get Chosen"

"**I**t just doesn't seem fair. When someone wants something so much that they can taste it, shouldn't they get it?

"I honestly feel like I deserved this, but they told me I need more experience. Well, how am I supposed to get experience if they won't even give me a chance? I could show them how well I can do, but I need the opportunity.

"I honestly felt I was as good as any of those girls up there. Maybe I'm not. Maybe I'll never be good enough. Every time I try to say, 'Hey, this is me, and I'm good at something,' I blow it. It happens every time. I start out feeling confident and secure, but somewhere I go wrong. Why does my confidence and security fade and my shyness and fear pop out? If I knew I'd do something about it, so maybe one day I'd be able to do it right.

"I'm *so* sick of being rejected. They say that rejection is part of reaching a goal, and if you can't deal with that, you're not cut out for that goal. But how many times does a person have to get rejected? I swear, as many times as I've been disappointed, part of me wants to just give up, while another part of me gets more and more determined.

"I *hate* dealing with disappointment. It's the worst feeling. You work so hard and try so much. You give it everything you can, and for what? Absolutely nothing. You just get let down after all that work. Why even bother trying? It's not worth the pain and suffering."

"I Hate to See Her Discouraged"

"Why won't they give her a chance? She keeps trying, sometimes after prodding from me, only to be disappointed again and again. It hurts to see her be rejected and to watch her self-confidence go down the tubes.

"I'm afraid she'll give up. She's got so much to offer, but how many times can a person take rejection before they start to believe that they just don't have what it takes?

"She's young, though. I'm so proud of her for taking the risk to try. I think there are a lot of kids out there who are so afraid of failure and rejection that they don't even attempt anything new. If she keeps giving it her best shot, I know it will pay off for her someday.

"I'm also proud that she has set goals for herself and is willing to pursue a variety of interests. How sad it would be if someone with her talents just sat in front of the t.v., waiting for life to deliver happiness to her doorstep.

"I just hope she doesn't get too discouraged. I know there

are times when she feels really self-confident and other times when she just wants to hide. The disappointments are hurts that I can't bandage like a skinned knee.

"I guess part of growing up is realizing that we don't automatically get what we want in life. For most of us it takes a lot of work. But I want her to know that if she doesn't get discouraged and keeps working, she will achieve what she wants.

"I hope she'll continue to work toward her goals. I strongly believe in her abilities, and I'll support her every step of the way. I really am so proud of her."

Cherishing the Effort

Teenagers feel very vulnerable as they attempt new goals and try to gain recognition for their talents. As we've discussed before, because this stage is the transition from childhood to adulthood, teens often aren't sure who they are. They tend to be hypersensitive to failures and rejection, taking them too much to heart.

Adults who have had a chance to experience some successes have learned that a failure doesn't indict them for life—there are always other chances. Teenagers, however, can be very susceptible to outside influences, and they can overreact to a single rejection. If someone gives them the message, "You're not good enough," they can interpret this as reality, not feeling sure enough of themselves to argue. Worse, they can generalize the rejection and believe it means they are worthless as human beings.

When a daughter faces rejection or failure in attaining a particular goal, a big factor which can influence how she will deal with the disappointment is her mother's reaction.

When children are small, parents are like gods, determining their reality. From their parents they learn the answer to
questions such as: "Is the world a safe place or not?" and "Am
I loveable or not?" As children grow up, they take these
lessons with them. With this in mind, mothers need to ask
themselves: "Has my daughter been taught that undertaking
new quests is good, regardless of the outcome? Or has she
learned that failure makes her less loveable?" (It is true that
as children grow into teenagers, parents become much less
godlike, but old lessons die hard.)

Mothers should consider what they have taught their
daughter about success and failure, and how safe it is to try
new endeavors. When a daughter has attempted a goal that is
dependent on outside recognition, such as auditioning for a
play, a band, or a talent show, or applying for a job, an award,
or a scholarship, mothers can encourage her effort while
teaching, through their own behavior, not to be too attached
to the results. This is the best way to keep from drowning in
disappointment when we don't "make the grade" as defined
by some outside source. Doing the best we can and letting go
of the results is definitely the way to go. If we get it, great. If
not, it has nothing to do with who we are. It may mean we
need to practice more, work harder, or prepare more, but it
should never mean that we don't try again.

If mom pushes her daughter toward goals that are more
in keeping with the mother's interests than the daughter's,
she is setting her daughter up for failure. It is important for
mom to ask herself (and her daughter) if this is the case. Is the
goal one that the daughter truly has for herself, or is she
doing it to try to please mom or dad. She may need to be given
permission to answer this question honestly by assurance
from mom that she would never want her daughter to go

through the striving and periodic disappointments of working towards a goal unless it was something she really wanted for herself.

A daughter has two choices when she doesn't quite make it. One is to give up, which results in narrowing the scope of her life as she slowly restricts her efforts to areas where she feels perfectly safe. The other is to bounce back, learn from the experience, and be willing to do what it takes to do better the next time. Not getting selected for something we really want is disappointing, so we should allow ourselves to feel disappointed for a while, and not deny the feeling. We just don't want to get stuck there. We can still go forward.

Mothers can celebrate their daughter's efforts. If the daughter has tried hard for something and still not been chosen, or somehow failed to attain some goal, Mom can reinforce how super it is that she tried by giving her special recognition for the effort. She can take her daughter out to dinner, lunch, or shopping, or give her a toast at dinner. Any time a teenager is brave enough to risk rejection in the process of reaching for a goal, she deserves a great deal of credit.

Friends

"Everybody Else Is Doing It"

"When you're part of a group and they do something that *everybody* but you seems to think is okay, what possible reason could you have not to do it too?

"One answer to this question might be because you think it's wrong. But what if I don't know if it's wrong? I'm not God. Who am I to say, 'Yes, that is morally and ethically correct,' or, 'No, you shouldn't do that?' And if all of my friends think it's okay, I don't see why I can't live a little and have some fun. After all, I'm a teenager, and these are supposed to be the best years of my life.

"But then there is that little part of me reminding me that all of my life I've been taught not to go along with the crowd. But if I stand back and just watch all my friends do something without joining in, they'll never really think of me the same way again. In fact, I wouldn't be surprised if I lost all of my friends. Then I'd know that being careful wasn't worth it, not with all my friends gone. Still, mom keeps telling me to be my own person, even when it's hard to say no.

"I look at how happy my friends are. They don't seem to be suffering a bit from any of their decisions. Their lives seem perfect. Maybe if I let them guide me, my life would be perfect too. I know I'd be a lot more popular than if I decided not to follow their lead.

"This is so hard."

"The Silent Voice"

"I guess I always knew that the older she became, the less influence I would have over her life. I just didn't think my influence would disintegrate into utter nothingness!

"Until recently, I felt that she at least considered what I had to say on important topics like sex, drugs, values, and long-term goals. Now I feel that the best thing for me to do is to keep my mouth shut. If I'm for something, she seems to take the stand against it. If I'm against it, she argues for it with a fervor that would make any politician jealous.

"Her opinions seem to be very much shaped by her friends. It's like they've formed an invisible communication network that hovers around her all of the time, and my opinions are filtered through those of her friends. They seem to be the ones who determine her attitudes and behaviors at this point.

"Sometimes I'm afraid she is so caught up in this network that it becomes more like a web—one in which she is stuck like a butterfly. Maybe in her heart, the values we've tried to teach her attempt to spring her free so that she can fly in her own direction, but the stickiness and strength of the web keeps her trapped.

"Her fate seems so precarious at times. Who is determining the direction of this group which influences her so much? Some are kids I don't know well, but some I know well enough to be frightened. If she follows the crowd just to belong, it could result in some irreversible mistake. Are they all having sex? Pregnancy or AIDS could be the consequence. Are they all using drugs? Addiction, an overdose, or trouble with the law could be the result. Are they all drinking? It only takes one drunken driving accident to take my daughter away from me forever.

"I want to release her from the web, but how can I? I want to remain an important voice in her life, but only she can decide whether to listen."

Being True to Oneself

The power of the peer group is a force that is experienced by most teenagers. It is a challenge that at some point, every teen must confront. In this case, to what extent should a daughter compromise herself in order to belong? At what point does she have to take a stand, alone if need be?

For many reasons, peer pressure is to be expected. As mentioned earlier, teenagers are unique human beings on the earth and it is very understandable that groups of them band together to form a sort of society of their own. And as in any group, leaders emerge, and others establish their own positions: peacemaker, "yes man," rebel, and even scapegoat. The group becomes like a family. It provides a safe haven at a time when the teen's real family might not seem particularly sympathetic because of the family members' difficulty in adjusting to her transition into adulthood.

The peer group may support a teen daughter in a way that parents can't, if only because they aren't experiencing what she is at the same time. The daughter may doubt that mom can really remember what it was like "way back then" when she was a teenager. But Mary, Christy, Lisa, and Jason know what it's like *now*.

As a result of this reasoning, daughters may tend to defer to their group of friends for guidance.

How much influence the group will have is determined by several factors. First, is the daughter a leader or a follower? If she is a leader, she will heavily influence the opinions and attitudes of her crowd. If she is not a leader, the type of friends she is attracted to will provide some clues. Are they teens with values and goals similar to those that mom has tried to teach her? If so, the mother's opinions and values are still being heard by her daughter, but in a way much more acceptable to her. If not, the daughter may be trying to assert her independence from her family by gaining group support for her rebellious attitudes.

Next, how secure or insecure is the daughter? If she is very insecure, she will fall prey to any group who takes an interest in her, because the group temporarily fills the void created by strong feelings of inadequacy. If she has some healthy self-esteem, she may go along with the crowd only until a major difference of opinion occurs. Then her feelings of self-worth may be strong enough to allow her to say, "No, this is not for me."

Mothers can't deal with the problem of peer pressure by suddenly delivering a healthy dose of self-esteem to their daughters. By the teenage years, the basic belief that we are either valuable or invaluable people has been pretty much established—although not irreversibly.

Daughters who value themselves tend to make constructive decisions for themselves, displaying fairly good judgment. Those who do not believe they are valuable people are more inclined to make destructive decisions for themselves and to follow a crowd more blindly. It is like having two rings—one silver and one made of tin. Which one would you polish and put in a velvet case?

If a mother feels her daughter is becoming a victim of a negative group and may be in for some serious consequences, she must intervene. She needs to express her fears to her daughter, and if the two are so estranged that the daughter cannot be reached, counseling may be needed.

Regardless of the challenges, mom should try and maintain a connection with her daughter through these years when she naturally gravitates toward her peers. To do this mothers need to consistently listen and provide as safe and supportive an environment at home as possible. The stronger the family support can be, the less sticky the web of peer pressure will be for a teen.

Still, daughters may find themselves feeling caught in the web at times. The group of friends that was so supportive at one point in time can get such a hold on her that she may feel she can no longer make independent decisions without suffering serious consequences, such as being shunned or ridiculed. This fear can keep her from being true to herself, even when in her heart she disagrees with the group's beliefs, attitudes, or behaviors.

If this sounds familiar to a daughter, she should try to talk to her mother. She will need to know that there is someone outside of her peer group who will support her if she loses the group's approval. She needs an outside force to remind her that her values are right, and that she will come out ahead in the long run. If she feels completely alone, it will be harder for her to take a stand when the time comes.

I remember Julie experiencing this kind of situation as

early as sixth grade. There was one girl in the class that was the leader, *the* most popular girl. If you wanted to be popular you had to have her endorsement. Julie wanted to be accepted more than anything, but she realized pretty quickly that acquiring this girl's approval meant having to "cop an attitude." She had to get somewhat smart with the teachers and talk tough to the other kids. This behavior was very foreign to her, and she struggled with the dilemma. I was lucky in that she chose to talk to me about it, and I gave her my thoughts about the situation. Although she experimented with the attitude bit, in the long run she won this girl over by being strong enough to be herself.

Belonging to a group of friends who look out for you and care about your well being is a real blessing. But being stuck in a web of attitudes that control you and take over your own judgment can result in the loss of your individuality and self-respect.

—————————— "*!*"

"I Hate Having to Go to a New School"

"This is so scary. Starting a new school year is bad enough, but starting a new school year with no friends is even worse. I'm sure most people are going to be polite, but polite and friendly are two different things.

"I'm so used to my old group of friends—eating lunch with them, walking to class together, being obnoxious with them, going out on weekends as a group—and now that's all over. Every weekend I'll be sitting at home doing absolutely nothing. And who will I eat lunch with? That will just be a great way to make a first impression—to sit at a table all by myself while everyone stares and laughs.

"Why did we have to move? I want my old secure, happy life back. Sure, *some* changes, like a new haircut or a new boyfriend, can be good. But not starting your whole life over again from scratch.

"What if I don't fit in? I don't know how these people

dress, look, act, talk, or anything. What if I'm drastically different from them? God, why can't I just have my old life back?

"Everyone says I'll make new friends in no time. I wish I had their confidence. Making friends is really hard. I'm not the type of person who can just go up to someone and say, 'Hi, will you be my friend?' That's just not me. It's not that I expect people to come to me, but it takes so much time to get close to people.

"I know I have to be patient, but it's so hard when you're uncertain of the future."

"Fear of the Unknown"

"Well, we crossed the hurdles of accepting the move as a family and the physical relocation. But just when I thought the worst was over, I realized that moving was the easy part.

"In about three or four days, the furniture and our belongings are pretty much in place. I wish it was as easy to put the other parts of our lives in order. I feel bad for all of us. My husband is starting a new job with people he's never met. I am too, plus I really miss my best friend. My youngest just sits alone in front of the t.v., not knowing what to do with his free time. And my daughter is very depressed.

"I didn't realize moving would mean loneliness for all of us. I know it was the right decision, but it's hard to really imagine what life is going to be like when you leave everything behind except your family and the furniture. It's difficult for me to know how to help them deal with the changes the members of my family are going through when I'm struggling with the same ones myself.

"My daughter has to start a new school. I can imagine how scary that is. And there will always be some kid to make sure it doesn't go too smoothly. She probably feels like I do starting my new job. Everyone will be sizing me up, wondering if I am friend or foe, to be an aid or a threat. I'm not even sure what my job involves yet, so I'll go in truly at the mercy of people I have never met before. Will they tell me everything I need to know to be successful, or hold back some small but crucial piece of information? Like my best friend who is a great cook, but when she gives you the recipe for one of her dishes she always forgets (subconsciously I'm sure) one important ingredient, so it never tastes quite as good when you make it as when she does.

"My daughter has to go through the same thing, only worse. She hasn't had a chance to experience enough changes in her short life to know that things usually do work out. People *do* reach out. Friends *are* made. We *do* become a part of things.

"I wish I could take on that first day of school for her. Then she could go in the next day knowing the worst was over. I guess my crow's feet would be a dead giveaway, though.

"We'll get through this change; I know we will. And in a few months it will seem like a half-remembered dream. But for now, it's real, and it's hard."

The Family As a Support Group

M oving into a new neighborhood is tough on every family member. In addition to all the employment, school, and neighborhood adjustments, there are the people adjustments, too. Those tend to be the most frightening. The transitions involved in moving can really bring home the need that everyone has, regardless of age, to connect with other human beings.

How can families survive? By supporting each other. Everyone is going through similar traumas, though they may be felt more acutely by a teenager. Still, this disruption threads the family together with an experience common to all its members, and this may be one of the few times in the life of the family when everyone shares a similar experience at the same time. Each person must put on his or her battle fatigues and fight that first encounter, whether it is with a new job, a new school, or a new playground. No one can make the adjustment for anyone else—each one is on the front line of their own particular battle and has to take any hits themselves.

But the family *can* talk about the experience together. What small victories or setbacks did each member of the family face that day? It will help the teenager get through the adjustment period if she knows that she's not alone in what she is experiencing.

The family can form a sort of support group for each individual. A support group is formed when two or more people who are experiencing similar problems in their lives sit down and discuss their common issues. They gain strength from talking about them with others who have a pretty good chance of understanding what they're saying because they themselves have experienced the same or similar things. Some famous support groups that have been very successful are those of Alcoholics Anonymous, Alanon, and Families Anonymous, and there are many, many more. Talking about problems seems to put them in perspective, and when we share our feelings with someone who is experiencing the same challenge, there seems to be a strength which comes from knowing we aren't alone. Another advantage of support groups is that they present the opportunity for each of us to learn from others what works for them. In a family there is one other decided advantage: the sharing allows stronger bonding within the family at a time when everyone is feeling somewhat out on a limb.

It is important for mothers to ensure that their daughters' fears aren't minimized by the rest of the family. For a mother to say, "What's the big deal? It's just another school" simply confirms that she doesn't understand. Moms should remember a time when they were very scared of a job interview, or maybe even how nervous they were before hosting a dinner party. Well, that was "just a job" or "just a dinner party," but at the time the fear was as real as any she has experienced. What she *didn't* need to hear from someone back then was, "What's the big deal?" To a teenager, going to a new school *is* a big deal, and it doesn't help for someone else who isn't going through what she is to tell her it isn't. This only tends to make a teen feel it is wrong to have the feelings she is experiencing.

Daughters should try to talk about what it's like to go to the new school. The first day will probably be the hardest, but the adjustment of making new friends and feeling like she's a part of things takes a lot longer. They should also try to listen to what other family members are experiencing. On the surface, daughters may have trouble relating to the the first day of mom's or dad's new job, but if they really listen, they will discover similar challenges which they can probably relate to.

Daughters should take advantage of any opportunity that presents itself to invite a new acquaintance over to watch a video, sleep over, or come for dinner. Those first few social contacts are important, so mom should do her best to support these opportunities any way she can.

Daughters also might try to reach out to their mothers and other family members as they suffer through the tough times. Nothing is more healing than stepping out of our own pain to help someone else. Everyone needs some sympathy and understanding after a move.

"Everybody Hates Me"

"**J**ust because of one person, everybody is mad at me. It's so stupid! All the kids I thought were my friends are just followers. God, I'm so naive and gullible to believe these people cared about me.

"How can everyone get so mad at me for no reason? I didn't even do anything. I hate this. I have to walk down the halls, eat lunch and sit all by myself while watching all my former friends whisper. I know they're talking about me.

"It makes me feel so bad and embarrassed, because everyone looks at me like I'm some kind of freak. They whisper, they stare, they laugh, and it's all at me and I know it. This is the worst feeling in the world.

"It's pretty weird that just the other day all the people involved in this were laughing and sitting *with* me, and in just a couple of days I can become their worst enemy. I hate it.

"How could they do this? I hate not having any friends, but I don't want to apologize when I haven't done anything wrong. The only way to get them to like me again is to apologize for something I don't even think I did. And if they treat me like this for no reason, how do I know it wouldn't happen again?

"How could my 'friends' turn against me over something so stupid. Since they've done this, I don't even know if I want them back as friends. Sure, I don't want them to hate my guts and give me the silent treatment, but they're not the kind of people I thought they were.

"I want to end this. It's already gone on too long, and all I want is for things to be the way they used to be. But I don't even know what I want to do. Should I forgive and forget, or be mad forever? Most of all, though, I want to know how I can end this."

"Childish Games"

"Why do girls do this to each other? At this age it seems like they're not satisfied unless they're mad at someone. And right now that someone is my daughter.

"They're really giving her a rough time at school. It's like the little clique has made it their mission of the day to make her feel embarrassed, left out and alone. And what the heck can I do about it?

"She wants to know how 'friends' can act this way. I tried to tell her that they aren't real friends or they wouldn't treat her like this. But that's not what she wanted to hear. They are the only friends she has.

"She wants to know how to make it end. I have some thoughts on that, but I don't think they rent machine guns. Or more practically, maybe I should call their mothers and let them know how their daughters treat their friends. Yet I know she wouldn't want me to do that.

"She feels so alone, and I can't fill the void. She's confused, and I can't make sense out of the situation for her.

She's disillusioned, and I can't light the way. She feels low and worthless, and I can't boost her up. I love her so much, and I hate to see her hurt.

"I wonder if she has ever treated any of *her* friends this way? If so, it's a real lesson to know what it feels like to be on the other side. So if that's what she is supposed to learn from this, the lesson has certainly sunk in. It's time she should stop being hurt.

"My daughter deserves a friend who will listen and want what's best for her. Someone who would never make her feel like an outsider. Someone who would be sensitive to her feelings and would never try to build herself up by pushing my daughter down. I'd be that friend if she'd let me."

Toughening Up

I f any teenage girl makes it to adulthood without being "shunned" at some point by her friends, she ought to write to *Ripley's Believe It or Not*. As mentioned earlier in this book, because teenage girls tend to be unsure of themselves they often travel in groups and identify strongly with them. A girl's group of friends becomes extremely important as a barometer of worth and self-esteem.

Nothing makes a clique tighter than a common mission. And what mission brings a group closer than the blackballing of a member? This activity makes everyone else feel safe and secure that they aren't the one being cast out.

Of course, this mission cannot be completed without a victim. When the victim is her own daughter, however, a mother can feel confused. She wonders how sweet little Susie and Mary could have been having soda and popcorn in her family room one week and the next be placing "hate" calls to her daughter. She may feel angry over the injustice of it all, and helpless that she can't fix the problem. These are feelings that will be shared by her daughter a hundredfold.

There is a very valuable lesson that daughters can learn from this experience. *We can't please everyone all of the time.* The reality is that trying to please everyone all of the time is a no-win situation, so we might as well get out of that game. It's a hard fact for teenage girls to learn, but in some ways it frees them to use their energy in ways which are much more productive and creative.

Mothers can explain to their daughters about the insecurities of teenage girls and the fickleness of peer groups. They can point out the irrationality of the entire episode by discussing with their daughters what they supposedly did to deserve this treatment. The answer is probably nothing—there is seldom any rhyme or reason. Therefore, trying to win these friends back doesn't make much sense, since there was no real reason for them to have dropped her in the first place. She can only wait out the situation.

Mothers can suggest that their daughter reduce the length of her banishment by pretending to be as unaffected as possible. The look of embarrassment, humiliation, and utter misery actually feeds the "shunning" because it is a sign of how successful the mission is. If there is no visible sign of success, the mission becomes boring and will soon be forgotten. Things then go back to normal, as the girls relent and eventually forget what they were supposed to be shunning the person for anyway.

Acting carefree in such a situation is hard for anyone to do. A daughter will have to muster up all the acting talent that she has. But her efforts will be successful.

Daughters should also try to talk to their mothers about how it feels, so they can release some of their frustration, anger, and sadness. If mother is insensitive to how much it hurts, the daughter should make her best effort to sit her down and explain.

In the meantime, mothers can guide daughters so they can take notice of some important lessons. One is that there is a difference between real friends and people in our social circle. This is the difference between diamonds and rhinestones—one is precious, the other just seems to be.

The second lesson is that we don't always get what we deserve, so it's up to us to make the best of it.

A third lesson is that maybe we as individuals ought to decide if we're worthwhile or not, rather than handing over the critical verdict to those whose opinions blow with the wind.

Mom needs to listen and accept that although in the adult world this situation may seem trivial, it is a major emotional crisis for her daughter, one that she has to face every day until it is resolved.

Love

"Is This Love?"

"I can't tell exactly what it is we have. We do so much together, and I feel so much for him. I think he feels the same for me. He is so good to me—he shows me he really cares in so many ways. And I do the same for him.

"I've never felt this way about any other guy. I've never experienced love, so I don't know what it feels like. I know I really care about him, but it's confusing. I love everything about him—his looks, his laugh, his walk, his personality, his sense of humor, everything. But I don't know if I'm "in love'"with him. I'm just not sure what that is supposed to feel like. When we talk about it, he's just as confused as I am.

"This is the most intense relationship I've ever had, and I'm so happy. People always say we are so perfect for each other and we feel like we are so perfect together. But is it too perfect to be love? Just what exactly does love have to involve?

"I feel like I need to know just what it is we share for a lot of reasons. I feel so much that it almost scares me, because I don't know just how real this is. If it isn't real, I'm anxious about allowing myself to feel too much, because I could get hurt. But if this is love, I should allow myself to feel as much as possible.

"Another thing is sex. People always say that if you are going to do something as serious as that, you have to make sure you love the person and that you are both responsible. I know we both would take responsibility if something went wrong, but is he the right person? How do I know? Sometimes I feel that if I was ever going to so something like that, he's the exact type of person I would want to share it with. But then at times I don't know if it's right or not.

"Love comes along so seldom and maybe this is meant to be. Then again, maybe it isn't. Maybe we just care about each other a lot and we just think we're in love. I don't know. But if we're not in love, why do I feel so much?"

"She Can't Be in Love"

"My little girl who still sits on my lap when the going's tough wants to know if she's in love.

"Love. Is there any word in the English language that has so many meanings? What she is experiencing could be a kind of puppy love—but I guess that applies more to crushes in elementary school. O.k., maybe it's an 'attraction.' But I guess it's beyond that, since they have been dating a while. How about 'caring?' Well, I guess that's how she feels about her fish. 'Liking a lot?' I suppose that's how she feels about her best girlfriend. 'Infatuation' may be closer. At least I _choose_ not to believe she's in 'real' love. That really scares me.

"Love to me means a strong possibility of sexual activity, and marriage. Now, I know she won't marry the first person she thinks she's in love with, but she's not going to marry anyone she doesn't think she loves, either. So, who knows? The sex thing scares me the most because I'm afraid she'll get pregnant, or AIDS. Either would bring an abrupt end to the goals she has set for herself, and, yes, the dreams _I_ have for her as well.

"There's a part of me that wants her to experience the joy of being in love. It certainly makes the world a brighter place in which to live. But there's part of me that wants to hold her back. *'Not yet, my love. There's plenty of time. Have fun, enjoy, and don't get too serious.'*

"There are two sides of love. One she is aware of now—the high, the joy, the elation. But I'm not sure anything can hurt as badly as the other side—the inevitable conflicts with someone you care so deeply for. I don't want her to hurt, not ever. But loving means risking and becoming vulnerable. I don't like it when she is vulnerable to pain in a world where I can't move in to protect her if needed.

"It's hard to face the fact that she is growing up so fast. Her learning about love really brings that home. I can only sit back and hope that I can catch her if she falls."

Love's Elusiveness

Julie once asked me the question, "Do you think this is love?" after she had been dating a boy three months. My natural inclination was to smile (patronizingly, I'm afraid) and to explain that she is far too young to even think she is in love, so let's just move on to the next subject, thank you. Looking back, I'm glad I bit my tongue, because that kind of response would probably have ended the discussion and would have widened the perceived (or perhaps real) gap where my daughter is convinced that I do not understand her.

Daughters in this situation are thinking, "If you could feel what I'm feeling you would know, Mom." But they are afraid that mom will mock them, and that their powerful feelings will be scoffed at by some statement which basically boils down to, "Don't be silly, dear."

The feelings of attraction that teenage girls feel to boyfriends are powerfully strong. If the feelings were coupled with more experience and a stronger sense of who they are, most mothers would call it love. As an adult, I know if I was single today and felt as strongly for a man as I did about any of the boys I thought I couldn't live without as a teen, I would definitely call it love.

What moderates the intense feelings, however, is the lack of life experience and the ever-changing and evolving nature of teenage girls. What the daughter feels is a definite attraction for a boy. It is important for her to experience this feeling, and to pursue relationships with those to whom she is attracted. Only then can she learn to distinguish the variety of feelings that attraction includes: admiration, infatuation, lust (I can hear the mothers reading this say "God forbid"), and love. She needs to experiment with different ways to express caring for another person, and to learn where to set boundaries. She will receive various responses from those to whom she is attracted, which will help her learn what results in her feeling special and valued. Daughters will, in time, learn to separate the real from the false.

Who the daughter is today is different from who she will be tomorrow, and what attracts her in the opposite sex will also change. She will learn from each relationship as she comes to know the real people behind the gorgeous "pecs," teeth, or eyes.

Only through experience do any of us learn that some powerful attractions don't last forever. As a matter of fact, they often don't last six months—sometimes not even three. Daughters will learn to differentiate their feelings with experience and come to trust that time will tell whether they have found a lasting relationship.

Mothers can listen to their daugthers and validate that what they are feeling now seems powerful enough. They can share their own experiences (in a positive way) of thinking they were in love and actually being in love. Mom can assure her daughter that her feelings will be sorted out with the passage of time, and encourage her to enjoy the relationship for what it is now without trying to define it.

Meanwhile, a mother needs to be patient. She may be praying that it's not love because she thinks the best thing the boy has going for him is the fact that he has clean ears. Yet if she tries to control the relationship by criticizing the boy or minimizing the importance of this person to her daughter, there is a great risk. Teenagers must assert their independence somewhere—this is an established fact. If a mother tries to control her daughter when it comes to this relationship, it could provide the perfect vehicle for her daughter to assert her independence, and lead to a serious break between mother and daughter.

Daughters can help the situation by trying to accept the relationship for what it is at the moment. However, this is very hard to do. It is important for them to talk about the relationship with someone, because this helps in learning about the nature of love. If the daughter is a particularly private person, she may want to write her thoughts and feelings down as a way of trying to clarify the meaning of it all. Daughters should try to understand, however, that any serious relationship with a boyfriend causes terror for most parents. They are usually afraid that their daughter will not be able to get past the relationship to pursue long-term goals, and that she may be coerced into sexual behavior with serious consequences.

When I overreact on this subject due to my anxiety, Julie has learned to be very patient with me and let me get my fears right out on the table. Then she takes them one by one and talks to me about them. This really helps me let go of my sometimes imaginary fears which are often not based in reality. Then I feel freer to give her space to explore the relationship without my interference.

Whether or not it's love will be determined soon enough. Mothers should try to listen and let their daughters explore their feelings without fear of being belittled or having the importance of those feelings minimized. A daughter can be encouraged to enjoy the relationship for what it is today. Time will indeed tell whether it lasts.

"Why Doesn't He Call?"

"Why do I always seem to be the one who has to call *him?* He's always made it a point to call if he couldn't see me at least once a day. At least he used to. Lately, I'm lucky if I talk to him once a day, and if I do, it's because I call him.

"Is he tired of me? Sometimes that's the impression I get. It feels like he doesn't even want to talk to me anymore. But if that's the case, then why not? He *must* be tired of me. I didn't do anything, at least not that I know of.

"It hurts because I'm so confused. I feel like I don't know whether I'm coming or going with him. When we do talk (because I call him), he acts like everything is fine...like he still has lots of interest, and I start to think I'm going crazy. But then his actions speak louder than his words because he doesn't make the effort to call anymore.

"If he's busy, I could understand that. But every time *I* call and ask him what he's doing, he'll say he's watching TV or something general like that. That kind of stuff *never* used to keep him from calling me. I don't understand."

"Should I Be Happy or Sad?"

"I t looks like my daughter's relationship is cooling. Talk about mixed feelings!

"In many ways, I'm glad. I hate to see her tied up with one boy when I know there are so many she needs to get to know if she is going to make a good decision regarding marriage. I know I'm jumping the gun, but every time she dates a new boy I can't help but imagine what her future would be like if she married him. I picture myself as the mother-in-law; what kind of a husband he would be; what their children would look like. Would he interfere with college? Sometimes I think I'd feel the safest if she never dated anybody more than five or six times. Then I wouldn't have to worry about her getting too serious, or about a romance interfering with her goals.

"It really doesn't have much to do with the guy, either. True, there are a few I wish she'd dump sooner than others, but it really doesn't matter how many qualities he has. I still see him as a threat.

"On the other hand, I hate to see her insecure and hurt. I guess the best scenario would be for every boy she ever meets to fall in love with her and let her naturally decide to dump *him* after a few dates.

"But that's not the way it works. She cares a lot about him, and I fear he may be getting ready to hurt her. The guy must be a real fool to give her up. God, I wish she could just shrug it off and take the phone off the hook. She's got much better things to do with her time than to sit around and wait for the phone to ring.

"I could teach her the stupid games that boys and girls play. You know—play hard to get; pretend you don't care when you do; be nonchalant when you're dying inside. But I hate to. Right now her feelings are pure and she is willing to give them freely and openly. How sad it would be to tell her to hold them back and manipulate others with them.

"So, if he calls, I'll continue to be afraid. If he doesn't, I'll hurt with her."

Surviving Love's Ups and Downs

Maybe he isn't calling. Maybe he's suddenly too busy to talk. Maybe a date is cancelled. The ups and downs of love during the teen years are enough to make one dizzy!

A mother may become aware of what appears to be the cooling off of a relationship because the teen confides this fear, or because she is obviously depressed and is suddenly not spending as much time on the phone each day. It may be difficult for mothers to be completely empathetic, since they may "know" that this is probably not the boy that their daughter will end up marrying. Still, it is important for moms to remember that this relationship, here and now, is the most powerful and real relationship that their daughter has ever experienced, and the emotional fallout may be as significant to them as the breakup of a long-term relationship would be to an adult.

It is not helpful for mothers to downplay the importance of the relationship, to minimize their daughters' fear and hurt, or to take advantage of what appears to be a great opportunity to name all the things they disliked about the boy to begin with.

What *is* helpful is for them to listen compassionately and accept their daughters' feelings. A mother should avoid saying, "You shouldn't be so upset," because the fact is that her daughter *is* upset. Statements like this can cause daughters to feel even more alone than is to be expected in this tough stage of development. Mothers should try to accept their daughters' feelings as being real and significant to them. Their pain and confusion at this point *is* their reality.

Daughters need to share what is going on with them. If they appear depressed but won't say why, mom has to play twenty questions to find out what's going on. If she isn't aware that her daughter is having problems with a boyfriend, she may give up trying to help if the daughter insists that nothing is wrong. Although talking about it won't make the hurt go away, it *will* help.

Mothers should also encourage their daughters to regain control over their lives. Waiting around for someone to call puts her in the role of "victim." Teens can take control by becoming more involved with other friends and activities which serve as a distraction and may help avoid giving the impression that they are "needy." Boys *or* girls at this age are more likely to maintain interest in an individual if that person has a life. If all the teen does is make sure he or she is available for this person, the challenge is over, and chances are interest will diminish.

Finally, both mothers and teens should remember that growing up and learning about love means experiencing a series of relationships. Maybe it's over and maybe it isn't, but in either case, daughters should try to step out of the victim role until this has been determined. Action will result in greater self- confidence, while waiting will erode self-esteem. And if this relationship *is* over, then there will be a new one ahead.

"I'll Miss Him So Much"

"What am I going to do? I'm facing so many months without him. He's become such a part of my life—I'll feel like a part of me is missing. I don't think a day will pass by without me thinking about him. And I'm so scared. What if he doesn't miss me? What if we separate and because of all the time, he decides that I'm really not all that important to him?

"He'll probably have lots of girls crawling all over him. What if he can't control himself and cheats on me? I know I'm supposed to trust him, but I know him and I bet he'll cheat. He probably knows I'll be right here waiting for him no matter what, and he'll just go and see other girls just to be a jerk.

"And there is no way I'll know unless he tells me. There he'll be, knocking himself out with all kinds of fun and there I'll be waiting, worrying and wondering. I know I just shouldn't care and I should just go and have a good time without him, but I can't. He's become so important to me that it seems like I can't really be happy without him. I think about him all the time. If I'm not thinking about the things we've done, I'm thinking about the things he's probably doing without me.

"Why am I letting myself do this? I don't want to be unhappy, but I can't help it. I want to be able to go out with friends and continue on with my life, and I know I will go out. I'm just not so sure it will be the same without him. Things won't be as fun, places won't be as interesting.

"It's a mixture of feelings. I'm scared, I'm depressed, I'll be lonely, and if I lose him, what if this feeling never happens to me again? I've never cared this much about anyone. What happens if he leaves, I never see him again, or things die, and I never find anyone I care about that much again? Sure, we'll write and maybe phone each other, but is that enough to keep a relationship going?"

"Helpless Again"

"God, I hate to see her sad. Her boyfriend hasn't even left yet and she's already depressed. I guess the reality is really starting to hit her as the time approaches. Both of them have been blissfully in denial of 'doomsday' (the day he leaves), which in many ways makes sense. It would be silly to spend the last few weeks together depressed because of the inevitable separation.

"I wish I could take away her fears and assure her that he will be true and this love will last forever. But the truth is that they are both so young that they each will probably meet other people. That's really not what she wants to hear, yet for me to perpetuate this hope on her part that the separation will not affect the relationship would not help her. Feeding this dream would only set her up for an even bigger disappointment than she might have if I said nothing one way or the other. I wish love were simpler for her—for all of us, for that matter.

"If I'm perfectly honest, there's a part of me that will be

relieved when he's gone. She'd never understand that if I told her. But she's so young to get serious and be tied down. If I could choose a state of being for her at this point in her life, it would be free, light, and open to all new adventures and possibilities. Later, when she is older, I pray that she will get the opportunity to experience the joy that comes from a committed, loving relationship, but I hate the thought of her cloistering herself like a nun while he's gone.

"Most of all I want to take away her fears, but I can't. I know she has to experience this separation as it unfolds, and I cannot protect her in any way. Sometimes I think the hardest part of motherhood is having to witness the growing pains of my children."

Patience

Witnessing the heartaches of daughters as they gain experience with love can cause a true feeling of helplessness for mothers. This feeling is one of the consistent struggles mothers experience, because they are starting to let go—voluntarily or not—and the teen has to swim pretty much alone in the waters of adulthood. And as anyone who has learned to swim knows, an aspiring swimmer has to go under the water and even swallow a mouthful of water a few times before the necessary skills are achieved. Daughters who are entering the world of love and intimacy have to struggle, feeling lost and confused at times, as they experience the joys and pains of learning to love.

If a daughter has developed deep feelings for someone who is leaving for whatever reason, there is one hard fact that even a mother can't change: goodbyes hurt. It is important to accept the fact that they are one of those times in life when one must experience the sadder side of being human.

However, this is an experience that allows a daughter to

learn that she can survive the sadness, and that sometimes the pain is actually worth the risk one takes to love. The important thing is the experience of loving. Most mothers would not choose for their daughters to never know love just to protect them from being hurt. The joy and fulfillment of love is definitely worth the pain.

Daughters will need quiet support in the form of listening and hugs. Mom can validate the sadness and encourage her to just allow the feelings to be there for a while. She has experienced a loss, and it is normal for her to mourn. Mothers may have to remind themselves, however, to actually allow daughters this depression, possibly feeling impatient for them to get on with their lives.

Trying to hasten the mourning process by minimizing the loss in any way is not a helpful tactic for mothers. Saying something like, "You'll get over it, darling. You only dated him six months," convinces a daughter that mom really doesn't understand, and probably never will.

A teen may appear to be self-centered for a few days as she grieves. The mother should try to accept this state for a time, because her daughter is putting much emotional energy into the healing process. And that is the goal, isn't it—to heal?

It will be very tempting for mom to encourage her daughter to go out and reengage her social life. Gentle suggestions which are mentioned and then left alone are fine, but mom should be careful not to push. It is really best not to interfere with the natural healing process.

Mothers should be particularly careful not to push their daughters to date other boys. They will date when they're ready, and pushing them sets the mother up as a perfect target for the anger resulting from being abandoned by their boyfriends. He's not there to take it out on, so the next most likely recipient is someone very close. To avoid becoming the person upon whom her daughter vents her anger, it is best for the mother to allow her some space and not to push.

When she's ready to revive her social life, there will be signs. She will either just "go out" with someone and mom will find out after the fact, or she'll drop subtle hints, such as a compliment about some boy or by telling her mother something about him. (Mothers should try not to be too obvious when they jump for joy.)

Daughters need to confide their feelings of sadness and loss in someone who will listen and accept them. If mother is trying to minimize the experience, the daughter should attempt to understand that her mother is trying to help her.

Believe it or not, most parents don't know how to help their teens deal with their emotions. Unfortunately, there isn't a class you can sign up for in high school or college. I can honestly say I learned almost everything I know from Julie's coaching. She would say things like, "Mom, don't tell me it will go away. That doesn't help me. I feel this way *now*." Or, "You can't make it go away, Mom, so please just listen and hold me." Daughters know what they need from their mothers at times like these, and most mothers would appreciate their help. Reading minds is pretty risky business.

"He Cheated On Me"

"How could this have happened? I thought everything was going just fine, and then he pops up with one of those, 'Oh, by the way…' kind of things. Like I'm supposed to think this is no big deal and just brush it off as nothing!

"If I just wasn't good enough for him and he had to turn to someone else, he should have sat down with me and told me that there was a definite problem and explained what it was. But no, he handles it by going out with some other girl. If he thinks that I'm just supposed to forgive him and not think anything of it, he is way too high on himself. I think what he did is really wrong, and he should think so, too.

"How could he do this to me? This girl had to really be great if he'd hurt me like this. But then again, maybe she isn't so great—maybe I'm just not good enough. But why not? He makes me perfectly happy, and I honestly thought it was mutual. He really had me believing that. I suppose I must be way too gullible, since I actually believed someone who is obviously just a liar.

"What am I supposed to do? Do I tell him he broke my heart and I don't want to work it out? I mean, that would be locking him out of my life, and I'm just not sure that I want to do that.

"What about all the effort I've put in to make this relationship work? Was it even worth it? Should I say, 'O.k., I'll forgive you this time but don't let it happen again?' Yeah, sure. If it happened once, it can happen twice. And since this happened in the first place when I didn't even know we were having problems, what's to keep it from happening again? This is so hard. Why does love hurt so much?"

"A Mother's Wrath"

"**S**he seems really angry, but I think she's hurting—a lot. She was so happy and trusting in her relationship, and now she's been burned. Is it any wonder that people learn to play games with each other? When you give honestly, openly, and trustingly, you put your heart right out there for someone to pounce on with spiked shoes.

"I'd like to take that boy and jump on *him* with spiked shoes. Just end it, dammit, if it's over—don't betray her. I want her to experience the positive side of love, and this will only teach her to be wary and afraid.

"She may decide to go back with him anyway. That scares me, because she might decide to give him whatever it takes to keep him. If he says he cheated on her because she wasn't enough for him, how willing will she be to do whatever he wants out of fear he will cheat again?

"Love can be so superficial at this age. Like that song lyric, 'If you can't be with the one you love, baby, love the one you're with.' What a philosophy.

"I don't want her to cheapen herself to meet the fickle needs of any boy. I want her to know that what she brings to a relationship is special, and can't be substituted so easily by someone else.

"But she really cares for the jerk. (I'm sorry, but anyone who would hurt her this way has got to be a jerk.) I know it's not mature to get into name calling, but when it comes to seeing my little girl hurt, I don't feel like being so very mature.

"I hope she realizes how special she is and decides she just doesn't deserve to be treated this way. I hope she can cut her losses and move on, holding her head high. Maybe she could even feel sorry for him because he threw away a great relationship for a spur of the moment thing.

"She can learn from this. There will be many boys and eventually men in her life. Some are trustworthy, honest, and sincere; some aren't. She will learn from experience to differentiate between the two. It's a necessary lesson to learn in love.

"I guess forgiveness is possible, too. If she chooses to forgive him, I'll support her...this once. But God help him if he hurts her again."

Reality Testing

H ere is another example of a time when mothers have to sit back and allow their daughters to flounder a bit as they learn to swim in the waters of love. Fickleness and impulsiveness are fairly predictable behaviors for many teenagers. Boys and girls tend to be very changeable at this age, not knowing for sure who they are or what they want. For that reason a long-term commitment doesn't usually work out for teens. The two people in the relationship are changing so fast that it is easy for them to go in different directions within a short amount of time.

Maybe she wants a macho type at first, someone who keeps her guessing. Then, if she gets burned, she might decide the artistic, sensitive male is more compatible with her. Maybe he wants a beauty on his arm one day, only to get bored the next and decide that he prefers someone who shares more of his interests. Any day either of their hormones could lead them in opposite directions. All of us, at one time or another, have to experience consequences so we can learn to think an action through before jumping into it. Unfortunately, some teenagers, like some adults, never learn this lesson.

A mother can't take away the hurt, but she can lend a compassionate ear. First of all, she can help her daughter establish whether both parties ever agreed that the relationship was to be exclusive. Unfortunately, sometimes we feel strong feelings for someone and in our heart make a commitment, simply assuming the agreement is mutual. The possibility that a false assumption has been made should be explored.

It's important for a mother to let her daughter talk about the problem. The issue of how much to compromise oneself for the sake of keeping the relationship intact should also be discussed. A teenage girl can be vulnerable to pressures to go overboard to please her boyfriend, thinking that if she could make him *really* happy, he wouldn't cheat again. But whether the indiscretion consisted of a kiss, a date, or sex, he didn't think about her feelings. He did what felt good to him at the time. A mother can ask her daughter: "Do you want to stay in a relationship with someone who would take a chance on losing you for a short-term fling?" The other girl met his momentary need, whatever it was, but did he stay with *her?* Mom can point out that there is much more to a relationship than meeting each other's immediate "needs." She can also ask her daughter about what she thinks she deserves in a relationship. Does she deserve to be cheated on? Does she deserve to have her trust broken?

Daughters should talk about their feelings. It's very disappointing to find out someone you trusted cheated on you, and anger, frustration, and sadness can build up if they are not expressed.

Perhaps he has never done this before, and she wants to give him another chance. There are times this might be appropriate, if she thinks she can come to trust him again, and as long as she doesn't fall into the trap of compromising herself to keep him.   Another option is to date him as well as others for a while. That way, time will allow the feelings to sift down to what they really are, and she will know whether the relationship is based on convenience, security, habit, attraction, lust, infatuation, or love.

Mom can remind her daughter of how special she is. Being cheated on can land a hard blow to a person's self-esteem. A daughter may need mom to help her see that this episode has nothing to do with her self-worth, and to help her remember that she is a very special person.

"I'm Not a Baby Anymore"

"Doesn't my mom think it's about time she accepted the fact that I'm growing up? I have. Part of growing up involves sex. It doesn't matter what culture or religion is involved, a person is eventually going to have sex.

"It would be really easy for me to go and have sex because *I* think I'm ready, but I really don't think that's what she wants. Then again, maybe it is. Maybe she would rather not know, because she doesn't want to deal with this part of me. Maybe she'd just like to go on pretending that I'm still a little girl, even though I'm five feet eight inches tall.

"But I don't believe that. I think she would much rather have me come to her beforehand to make sure everything is taken care of and that I've acted responsibly, rather than have me come to her in a couple months and say, 'Well, I've been having sex for three months now, but I was afraid to tell you and now I'm pregnant.' I wouldn't want that for *my* daughter, and I don't think she wants it for me.

"Nobody, no matter who it is, can tell me when I'm ready

except me. So my mother shouldn't even try, because she really can't know if I'm ready or not. If she disagrees with my decision, that's fine, and she has the right to say that, but she also needs to understand that I have to make my own decision. And to trust me. I know she must have *so* much trouble trusting me, especially since this decision is mine alone to make, but she has to trust my judgment. And if I'm wrong, nobody will pay for the mistake but me.

"The only thing I ask from her is that she be there for me no matter what. I think I'm ready, and I'm trying to be responsible for my decision. I will eventually have sex with or without her approval, and she knows that. So isn't it better that I tell her, no matter how she feels about it, so that the two of us, together, can prevent any mistakes?"

A Mother's View

"She's Too Young"

"Someone should create a place where mothers can hide when they simply can't deal with what's going on at a particular time—a place where time stands still and everything freezes until they are ready to come out and deal with a situation.

"Well, the situation I'm facing right now is that my daughter is talking about having sex. This moment, which I suppose I knew would arrive someday, scares me more than anything we have ever faced together.

"She thinks she's ready to have sex. She's just a teenager! Our definitions of a committed relationship are so different. She thinks dating someone for six months is a guaranteed sign of a committed relationship. I was thinking more along the lines of three or four years.

"Why does this scare me so much? I don't think it's visualizing her in the actual act that bothers me the most. I mean, it *is* uncomfortable, but not terrifying. I think what I'm most afraid of are all the possible consequences that accompany having sex. I don't care how careful people are; girls (and women for that matter), *do* get pregnant unexpectedly. Even the pill isn't foolproof. Maybe 97% safe is good enough for some people, but it's not safe enough for my daughter as far as I'm concerned. And then I think about condoms. I've met too many women who laughingly say they should have named one of their kids 'Buster.' Those things break. (They'd have to be made out of two-inch steel to be completely safe in my book.)

"And if she did get pregnant there's the whole issue of what a teenager should do with a baby. Abortion may or may not be an option in her mind. If it is, it would be a tough thing for her to live with the rest of her life. And if she had the baby, what would she expect me to do? Babysit while she finishes high school? I've raised my kids and I don't want to raise hers or anyone else's. She says nobody but she would pay for any mistakes. That's not true at all.

"Then there's AIDS. One thing I know for sure is that once people cross the line and become sexually active, they seldom go back to being abstinent. If she starts having sex at such a young age, how many sexual partners will she have before she dies? The potential is pretty high, much higher than if she waited until she met the man she would marry, married him, and then had sex with only him until her dying day. That's safe—especially if she's on the pill and he uses condoms.

"I know I'm probably being unreasonable and unrealistic. Most women probably have sex with more than one man during their lives. But why start so early? She couldn't possibly know enough about men yet to have a good idea of what she wants and how to deal with the emotional fallout if it doesn't work out. I don't want her to feel ashamed that she chose to give herself to someone who then turned his back on her.

"My mind tells me to stay calm and face this like an adult. In my heart, though, I want to keep my daughter safe, and I'm scared because I'm starting to see that I really can't. Not anymore."

Woman to Woman

How the topic of sex is handled in a family is a very personal thing. The trouble is in many families it isn't handled at all. The subject is avoided, discounted, and postponed until the child has learned all the basics about sex from their peers—peers who usually don't know much about the topic.

Some parents are more comfortable than others with the sexuality of their teenagers. But no matter how they feel, there's no getting around the fact that it emerges in adolescence. Teenagers' bodies change almost overnight before their parents' very eyes. Their voices change as do their interests.

Parents can be very threatened by these changes which mark the erosion of parental power and control as their child undeniably transforms into an adult. (Some parents are more comfortable with this phase of development than others, and can celebrate the changes with their teenagers.)

A family's orientation toward sexuality can range anywhere from rigidly puritannical to openly permissive. Most mothers find themselves somewhere in between the two extremes. Regardless of their attitudes, however, there are a few guidelines that will help establish a meeting ground for mothers and daughters on what is for most of us a sensitive issue.

The truth is that a parent cannot scare a teenager into not having sex. The decision to have sex is more a function of development, emotions, hormones, maturity, and desire. As a result, statements on the part of a mother to scare her daughter into denying her sexuality just don't measure up against these other powerful forces for long.

A mother might begin to understand if she thinks back to what it was like when it was time to give birth to her daughter. Could anyone have scared her enough by telling her how painful it might be, or even by convincing her that there was a madman loose in the hospital, to keep her from giving birth? No. When it was time, it was time.

Fortunately, there are more than physical forces involved in the decision to have sex, and this is where mothers can positively influence their daughters' decision. But they should throw out the scare tactics. If she decides to remain a virgin until she marries, it won't be because she was scared into believing she could get pregnant from french kissing.

The "shame" approach is another way some mothers attempt to control their daughters' sexual activity. This strategy not only is fruitless in guiding sexual behavior, but also can create a barrier in the relationship between mother and daughter. Some examples of shaming statements are: "If you have sex with that boy, I'll never trust you again." "If I ever find out you've had sex, it will be the biggest disappointment of my life." and "If I ever find out that you've had sex, I'll never speak to you again." You get the idea. Sometimes these kinds of messages are communicated in a more subtle way than saying them outright, but are still conveyed. "Did you read in the paper that 50% of the sixteen-year-old students in your school are having sex? They must come from bad homes." The "shame" approach only convinces the daughter that the worst decision she could possibly make would be to go to her mother with questions concerning this issue—or any other issue, for that matter.

A mother can preach to her daughter until she's blue in the face not to have sex. This is a waste of words, time, and energy. What she needs to do instead is to create a environment where her daughter will be willing to honestly say what she is thinking and feeling on the subject. Creating such an environment might mean mom has to bite her tongue so she can listen instead of preach. It might mean that she has to dig her fingernails into her palm so that she doesn't just grab her daughter and try to lock her away in a closet.

Mom needs to listen and try to understand where her daughter's thinking is on the subject so she can meet her there. Only by relating to her daughter on *her* wavelength can she hope to have some influence on her decision because when two people are miles apart, they cannot hope to work together to resolve anything. Then, woman to woman, the two can discuss the pros and cons of becoming sexually active.

Mom needs to step out of her traditional role to some degree, because this isn't a "mommy to little girl" topic. This discussion should include the risks, both physical and emotional. It can also involve defining the goals the daughter has for herself at this point in her life and how an unplanned pregnancy might affect those goals.

Daughters who are able to go to their mothers to discuss this topic of sex are doing their mothers and themselves a big favor. It is hard to handle such a big decision alone, or with only the guidance of other teenagers, whose experience and perspective are somewhat limited. Mom can help her daughter look at both sides of this very important issue if her daughter is willing to be honest about her thoughts, feelings, concerns, and beliefs. This will not happen, however, if mom flies off the handle when her daughter approaches her on the subject.

Mothers should honestly share their fears with their daughters. (It may be hard for mom to accept the fact that her daughter is growing up, and she may resist facing this reality. But if her daughter is ready to face it, mom better get ready to do the same, because ignoring it won't make it go away.) She can tell her daughter what her fears are in the event of pregnancy and clarify how she might feel about getting cornered into raising another child.

If she still feels that her daughter is about to make a mistake after discussing the situation, mom can say something like, "I hope you will decide not to have sex yet for the reasons we've discussed. I don't think you are old enough to accept all the possible consequences. But you are the only one who can make that decision. No matter what you do, I want you to tell me. I will promise to respect and accept your decision even though I may not like it or agree with it. There are parts of your life now that I don't have any control over. I promise to support and help you any way that I can."

About the Authors

Julie Jordan is fifteen years old and a high school sophomore. She and mother Carol Koffinke live in Bel Air, Maryland.

Carol Koffinke has been a professional family counselor for the past sixteen years. She is the author of *I'll Never Do That To My Kids: The Parenting Traps of Adult Children,* which was published by Deaconess Press in 1991.